THE SILENT COMMUNITY

SOCIOLOGICAL OBSERVATIONS

series editor: JOHN M. JOHNSON, *Arizona State University*

•••••●●●•••••

"This new series seeks its inspiration primarily from its subject matter and the nature of its observational setting. It draws on all academic disciplines and a wide variety of theoretical and methodological perspectives. The series has a commitment to substantive problems and issues and favors research ana analysis which seek to blend actual observations of human actions in daily life with broader theoretical, comparative, and historical perspectives. SOCIOLOGICAL OBSERVATIONS aims to use all of our available intellectual resources to better understand all facets of human experience and the nature of our society."

— *John M. Johnson*

Volumes in this series:

THE SILENT COMMUNITY

Public Homosexual Encounters

by Edward William Delph

 SAGE Publications / Beverly Hills / London

For information address:

SAGE PUBLICATIONS, INC.
275 South Beverly Drive
Beverly Hills, California 90212

SAGE PUBLICATIONS LTD.
28 Banner Street
London EC1Y 8QE

Printed in the United States of America

Library of Congress Cataloging in Publication Data

Delph, Edward William.
    The silent community.

    (Sociological observations; v. 3)
    Includes bibliographical references.
    1. Homosexuals, Male—New York (City) 2. Non-verbal communication. I. Title. II. Series.
HQ76.2.U5D45   301.41'57   78-629
ISBN 0-8039-0990-X
ISBN 0-8039-0991-8 pbk.

FIRST PRINTING

CONTENTS

TO EVELYN, DARROW,
HARRY, and JON

Forword

Two men passing on the street may momentarily glance at each other, drop cues that each is homosexual and interested in the other, hesitate for confirmatory signals and, within a half hour, consummate their "spontaneous" love in the many available niches that are legion in congested New York City. Communicating erotic designs through a silent language of subtle cueing and posturing, these men make covert homosexual statements in and around everyday life in an attempt to generate dialogues of sexual intimacy. Undeterred by conventional expectations, identities, imagery, attire, and the like, the public homosexual eroticist cautiously probes existing conventional settings and situations for possible erotic liaisons while skirting negative sanctions. Erotic transactions also take place, of course, in settings that specifically encourage them, e.g., the homosexual bar and bath.

Public sexuality is integrated into ordinary life on an ongoing and pervasive basis with the unwitting and some-

9

times witting acquiescence of not only the police, whose job it is to control such enterprises, but before average citizens who are often present or nearly so during erotic episodes and who, if they perceived them, would be outraged. How is it that action considered immoral, and in this case abhorrently so, continuously takes place, not only in isolated settings like the gay bath on First Avenue and various hidden gay bars, but in the most pedestrian of places such as subway cars, streets, and public toilets? What are the methods of recognition, communication, and getting together in ambiguous, threatening, dangerous, and unfamiliar settings? Why are transactions always pursued in silence and anonymity? Are suspected others merely reacted to as "male" or is there a system of selection? If so, what is it and how is it managed in public?

Public sex seems possible because of (1) the types of stages utilized by the actors in conveying messages to suspected homosexual eroticists and the way in which setting features facilitate erotic identity statements and sexual actions; (2) the quiet cues in identifying fellow participants; (3) the craftsmanship in subtle communications; (4) the type of interaction that ensues; and (5) an ability to maintain conventional boundaries while engaging in exotic types of behavior. Time, physical layout, ecological placement (both spatial and moral), setting function, situational boundaries, social others, plausibility structures, knowledge, visibility, perception, risk, tolerance, and possible coercion are thrown into the potpourri of considerations in the placement of erotic endeavors as molded by these sexual entrepreneurs.

These entrepreneurs form a well-defined community of interest. Engaging in erotic behavior around the moral imperatives of society silence, impersonality, and anonymity prepare accessible pathways to erotic others with a good sense of security, evoking a strong sense of commitment to community participation. The gestural quality of cueing transcends situational contexts, forming a trans-situational, communal communications network.

This ethnography is an outgrowth of research done as a

graduate student at the New School for Social Research. I wish to express a deep appreciation to the graduate staff for their uncompromising scholarly excellence, with a special expression of gratitude to my advisors, Professors Arthur J. Vidich, Benjamin Nelson, and Marnia Lazreg. Without the understanding, patience, support, insights, and always encouraging criticism of Professor Vidich, this monograph would not have been possible. I also wish to thank Professor Stanford M. Lyman for his stimulating ideas, and to my Sage Publications editor, Professor John M. Johnson who provided invaluable assistance in the final preparation of the work. Lastly, and most importantly, special thanks to the thousands of nameless individuals who unknowingly shared their public adventures with me, providing the data for this work.

Edward William Delph

Introduction

For fully a century after our early social science founders advanced the radical idea that human actions could be (and should be) studied in a systematic or scientific fashion, there were virtually no empirical studies of sex or sexuality. Sigmund Freud, Albert Ellis, and Alfred Kinsey are among the courageous exceptions to this which come to mind. But such a situation obtained despite the obvious pervasiveness of sexuality in daily life. For intellectuals and scientists morally committed to probing and exploring "the fundamentals" of human existence, the paucity of empirical research over the course of a century appears strange. The situation probably resulted from a confluence of many factors, the cognitive-rationalist biases of the scientists themselves, the secrecy of sexual activities and feelings, the (historically narrow) moral norms of the scientific community, the (historically close) relationships between the scientific community and the state officialdom, and many others. A close reading of our social science literature tends to give one the impression that ideas, values, norms, attitudes, and beliefs are the prime-movers of human actions, but that

13

feelings about sex and sexuality account for very little of worthiness or importance.

All this has now changed. During the past 10 to 15 years we have been given an increasing number of rigorous and thoughtful empirical studies of sexuality and the various sexual scenes to be found in our society; and as we learn more and more our ideas and feelings about sexuality and its importance to our lives are beginning to change. Typically, these contemporary researches have been done by unheralded individuals who have, on many occasions, shown uncommon courage in pursuing and publishing their research interests. On many occasions they have had to pay a dear price for their commitments by being stigmatized by their local or professional communities, or both. Some have been jailed. Some have lost jobs. Others have suffered even more enduring and painful injuries in their lives.

We owe a great debt to these contemporary pioneers who have expanded the frontiers of our knowledge about human sexuality and its forms and meanings. They have had the tenacity and courage to leave the cloistered academic settings to venture forth and observe, record, and analyze human sexuality in the natural settings of daily life where it occurs, and to try and understand its meanings from the perspectives of those who participate. These studies include Albert Reiss' study of young streetcorner hustlers, Evelyn Hooker's researches of gay communities, David Ward and Gene Kassebaum's studies of the dynamics of homosexuality in prisons, William McKinstry's study of pornographic book stores and their patrons; Parker Rossman's study of pederasty, and Laud Humphreys' award-winning study of impersonal sexual encounters in public toilets (or "tearooms"). Others include Meredith Ponte's study of a homosexual drive-in, Martin Weinberg's studies of nudist camps, Paul Rasmussen and Loren Kuhn's study of massage parlor sex, Jerry Cloyd's study of heterosexual pick-up bars, Carol Warren's study of the male gay community, and Barbara Ponse's study of the lesbian community. Still others include H. Taylor Buckner's study of heterosexual transvestism, John Gagnon and William Simon's various empirical and theoretical inquiries of homosexuality, Robert Castle's study of a brothel servicing an airborne clientele, and Philip Blumenstein and Pepper Schwartz's studies of bisexuality in men and women. Also, Sharon and Phil Davis' study of the victims of "erotic offensiveness" (or flashing), Jack Douglas, Paul Rasmussen, and Carol Ann Flanagan's study of nude beaches, Charles Varni's study of mate-swapping, James Henslin and Mae Biggs' research on the sociology of the vaginal examination, Peter Manning's study of abortion-seekers, and Jay Corzine and Richard Kirby's study of sexual encounters among cross-country truck drivers. There are others as well. Taken together, these observational and ethnographic studies have greatly increased our awareness and understanding of contemporary human sexuality.

Edward Delph's *The Silent Community* represents a major contribution to our emerging understandings of sex and sexuality. It stems from an unconventionally long period of participant observational research —the kind where the observer seeks to integrate ones's self into the research settings in order to observe daily actions during their natural ebbs and flows — and Delph's observations began even before most of those of the aforementioned (already published) researches. In it he describes a variety of sexual activities which are consummated on a routine and daily basis in and around public settings of our large cities, including streets, public toilets, subways, gay bars, public parks, "piss-elegant bars," movie theatres, gay baths, "pig parlors," beaches, empty tractor-trailers, "meat racks," and public buildings. Such settings are usually known about in a given city, especially among those interested in using them to gratify their sexual or erotic desires, and the knowledge of the different uses made of these commonplace city spaces is what distinguishes the erotic community from the ordinary population.

The Silent Community is clearly no ordinary descriptive case study, one content merely in documenting that certain kinds of sexual activities take place in certain public places. Rather, it seeks to understand the nature of the social and sexual interactions which occur in settings where verbal utterances are virtually absent. It illuminates how individuals learn and use the special self-presentations, bodily posturings, gestural cues, the manners and informal (but sanctionable) rules unique to the settings; how the distinctive meanings of space, time, and manner (or "self") separate these erotic worlds from the conventional ones; how public sexuality produces a metamorphosis of the individuals who partake in it, thus transforming normal selves into erotic selves. Moreover, it sheds light on the question of why individuals engage in such potentially discreditable and stigmatizing actions, and some of the meanings for the participants.

In one sense *The Silent Community* contributes to the growing numbers of excellent observational and ethnographic researches we noted earlier; but in another sense this book embodies important questions which also inspired our classic social and political theorists —St. Simon, Tonnies, Hobbes, Marx, Weber, Durkheim, and many others — about the fundamental nature of human community and social order. In *The Sociological Tradition*, Robert Nisbet proposes that this very question is one of the major and recurring themes to be found in our Western intellectual traditions. Edward Delph's work fits in with this classical tradition of social thought, and draws its animating inspiration from a concern to understand the nature of the communal ties which bind individuals to one another, but it also departs from the classical tradition in an important and provocative manner. His proposition that those who engage in public eroticism and sexuality form a *community*, even one with an international membership, clearly represents an innovative divergence from the traditional conceptualization of community. It is clear that the "silent community" of which Delph writes is not a community in the traditional sense, where individuals are tied to one another largely through a commitment to the traditionally legitimized institutional forms, such as family, clan, church, work, party, and state. It would be wrong for us to think of community only in these traditional terms if there are facts which indicate otherwise.

And Delph's empirical observations do. From his view, eroticists *feel* a sense of community with one another. They share erotic desires to be sure, but they additionally share much more too. They share a common sense of being stigmatized and victimized by the general society. They share a common argot, and distinctive ideas about territoriality, persons, appropriate manner and demeanor, social time. Furthermore, as Delph points out in several of the following chapters, public eroticists are morally committed to the segregation of their actions from public view; indeed, the sense of adventure which obtains from the clandestine and secret nature of the actions is one of the exciting and motivating features leading to continued involvement for many of the participants, and it is in itself an important factor in the personal careers as public eroticists. This runs directly counter to the conventional wisdom in our society — which presumably underlies our laws proscribing such actions — that public eroticism (especially homosexuality) constitutes a public nuisance or a threat to the unsuspecting young. Public eroticists also have common enemies. It goes without saying that, if knowledge of the sexual uses of public places distinguishes the erotic community from the general population, then this knowledge may be used by those seeking to victimize or attack this community, notably hustlers, thieves, muggers, "fag-haters," and vice cops. Moreover, as Delph implies throughout the following chapters, while specific public eroticists do have their own personal preferences and do reject others on various grounds, these are idiosyncratic rather than patterned judgments of community members. Generally, the community of public eroticists is a surprisingly egalitarian one, and the traditional meanings of our societal status and prestige hierarchies largely dissipate in the actual settings of erotic conduct. Again, the important point of all this is that, according to Delph, public eroticists *feel* a sense of community with one another, and this is partly independent of individuals' feelings about their other (gay or heterosexual) social involvements.

The Silent Community is not a book about social change.

It doesn't really address the broader questions of how some officially proscribed activities may lead to the emergence of new and different social forms, or new communal bonds among individuals. Edward Delph is not chiefly concerned here with an analysis of the historical shift in the meanings of community which his chapters describe; but these questions are implied throughout. We will have to await further developments and the works of others to tell us whether such forms will prove viable or transitory, or whether they will be temporarily quashed by the legal apparatus of an insensitive and repressive general public. Because of this, perhaps it could be said that Delph's singular achievement is that his work has raised at least as many questions as it answers.

John M. Johnson
Arizona State University

chapter 1

A SILENT COMMUNITY[1]

WHO IS THE PUBLIC HOMOSEXUAL EROTICIST?

Is he the heterosexually married man followed home by an interested individual after both engaged in sexual activity on a subway?[2] Is it Dolly who swishes, lisps, and screams when with friends but adopts a severe, masculine self-presentation during frequent toilet adventures?[3] Is he Dr. E (see Appendix: On the Research Methodology) or Dr. P., an eye surgeon, both of whom spend hours upon hours in the trucks (see Chapter 2) acting out erotically? Is he the Baptist minister from Brooklyn who can be found every summer evening in the "meat rack"[4] on Fire Island? Is he the black shake-down artist who visits tearooms, gets "fucked in the ass," has an orgasm, and then rips off the insertor

because he knows that the latter will be too intimidated to call for help? And how about the young "studs" who actively cruise the johns, parks, beaches, and streets enticing overtures with erections and then physically abusing those who respond to them? Obviously the public eroticist is all of these and thousands of nameless others who appear sporadically on public erotic turf. The singular frame of inclusion that defines the public eroticist is that he can be discerned only after he wanders onto the public erotic arena and drops cues and clues about his sexual intentions. His departure deprives fellow eroticists, and any would-be onlooker, of finding him elsewhere.

The population shares two fundamental distinctions: they erotically act out in public and do so in a covert manner to avoid exposure or apprehension. They do, most importantly, actively pursue sexual objectives in public places. Not merely interested in "passing" and shunning stigma as a homosexual, locating desirable sexual others for erotic dialogues is a continuous and active preoccupation.[5] The fear of apprehension, embarrassment, social abuse, and other types of threats may constrain unfolding communications and interaction, but they do not deter the homosexual from prosecuting erotic endeavors.[6]

In addition to the public eroticist, there is a host of nonavailable and possibly hostile others who may be located in and around an erotic setting and who may be playing different games than the erotic one. The "co-presence" of such knowledgeable individuals complicates the cruising scene in the subrosa world of the public eroticist (Goffman; B1963: 17).[7] They consciously share the same frame of reference as the latter but for other than erotic reasons. For example, vice squad workers, muggers, fag-haters, knowing-but-not-caring witnesses, and mutually interested eroticists sometime occupy the same theater of action, creating an incredible mix of mirrors and masks in rapidly changing, and certainly confusing social contexts (see Bowers, 1972). Although small in number they prove threateningly troublesome. They know what is going on and know the game well enough to manipulate it for their own ends. As occasionally active participants and direct or indirect contributors to the sexual setting, they can dramatically affect an erotic situation and are included as part of the population under study.

Active, discernible erotic statements delimit a homogeneous population that fashion tangible claims upon the moral fiber of public settings. These disclosures represent immoral entrepreneurship of a singular kind. Joint adventures presume shared knowledge and include the risk of suffering a common fate if caught. To successfully posture erotic identities (that is, be actively and knowingly included in a sexual dialogue) and avoid detection, subcultural techniques of communication and involvement must be learned. Sexual posturing and activities unfold in special symbolic contexts, requiring the ability to see them. The transformation of normal identity into an erotic one requires a special form of social art. This metamorphosis simultaneously restructures the situation. Definitions, expectations, and modes of interaction evolve into an involvement not possible in other situational definitions and with other identities. The actors know the full round of implication that their erotic actions imply.

The preceding characteristics outline a specific and observable population, and an actual reality rather than one of social fiction. They reveal the perspective of the homosexual on the "make"[8] — that is, perceiving a situation as fruitful for sexual endeavors within the same frames of reference the public eroticist takes for granted. Because erotic communications afford easy, intimate access to and withdrawal from postured identities, they make for some ease in observation by the social scientist.

Those who define themselves as homosexual need not be part of the population who makes public sexual disclosures. It is equally possible that there are individuals who engage in public homosexual sexuality who do not identify themselves as homosexual. In the first instance, the self-identified homosexual need not disclose his identity in public. By abstaining from homosexual activity, seeking psychological aid, undergoing surgical transformation (the case of Agnes, in Garfinkel, 1967), or getting "married" to another homosexual, knowledge of their identity remains private (see Leznoff and Westley, 1963).

Reiss (1968) on the other hand, conducted a study of youths who sold sexual favors to fellators via the street. Not perceiving themselves as homosexual, they can be labeled as such if apprehended while selling their much sought after favors. They also occupy the very popular if nebulous status of "trade" in homosexual circles.[9]

THE EROTIC MOTIF IN PUBLIC ENCOUNTERS

The thread that binds this population together, and particularly distinguishes it, is the active erotic homosexual behavior in which they engage. The erotic includes actual, physical, sexual contact and the various, if somewhat obtuse, gestural communications defined as erotic by participants. Sexual definitions arise from the imputed and/or actual meaning complex of communications, including physical, biological and emotional responses. Imputed symbolic meanings are an integral part of these messages (see Parsons, 1951: 387). That is, when an individual accompanies looking at an erotic object by inserting his hands in the pockets of his trousers, the recipient of these significations assumes that the insertion intimates auto-manipulation of the genitals and an escalation in the erotic dialogue. The hands, however, may quietly rest within. It is the "looking" and the insertion of hands that magnify the sexual meaning and not necessarily obvious manipulation of the genitals.

Physical responses to sexual stimuli are readily apparent and feed into the communication network. Erections, auto-manipulation, tongue movement, and other gestures encourage identity conversation and hurry erotic transformation. The visual character of erotic messages occasion the capability of generating significant communications between actors without concomitant verbal communication. This creates a visible "social membrane," including all those to whom transmissions have been directed and excluding others who have been omitted from erotic significations. Erotic cues fashion a visible "gestural vocabulary of motives" between participants that preclude the necessity for verbal discourse and focus interaction on impersonal and anonymous grounds (see Mills, 1967).

The auditability of erotic dialogues (e.g., erections, groin rubbing, and hard stares) opens the possibility of establishing contacts in a host of dissimilar settings as long as intentions are masked and conform to expected contextual behavior (McCall and Simmons, 1966). The nexus between action and reaction gradually seeds an erotic topic in front of a presumed-to-be ignorant or presumed-to-be-tolerant host of social others.

The erotic serves therefore as the observable, perceivable element in public claims, the motivation behind these claims, and the topic and motif of interaction, the mode of communication within the situation, and suggests the problematics, and craftsmanship of mirroring conventional discourse while masking visible, emotionally charged and highly unconventional pursuits.

It cannot be determined whether those involved in such activities prefer them because they are public or whether, due to other personal life circumstances, they simply find themselves erotically acting out in public. There are many reasons that might motivate the individual to do so. Reiss' peers meet fellators for pecuniary rather than sexual reasons, while the fellators with whom they meet are interested in the sexual aspects of the liaison. The extraordinary tension due to the danger in some public settings may evoke participation (see Humphreys, 1970). Other individuals have little if no other means of adequate sexual expression (see Schofield, 1965, for a discussion of the "facultative homosexual"). However, members of the community come together on the assumption that each presumes the other wants sex. "Situational fix" of erotic identities and roles does not guarantee common ends. Bars and baths, blatantly sexual, could be arenas for imposters, blackmailers, and murderers, as well as for "mutual partners." One individual plys the toilets, for example, to commit robbery. He urgently presses for anal sex in order to go through the mark's wallet. If the public eroticist continually "games" society, the game he plays may be quite different for those with whom he shares it (Lyman and Scott, 1970). Whatever the game or social reality, the medium through which they communicate and come together devolves solely on the sexual.

The corpus of erotic cues and significations, the tangible data of highly amorphous and ambiguous dialogues contribute to an open-ended perspective through which social contexts and identities are probed and tested for reciprocal interests. An erotic world can be "manufactured" provided the "right" information seems apparent. The erotic becomes a universalistic perspective that invites immediate physical access if cues and clues establish sexual parameters within reasonable limits of doubt. In contexts reputed to cater to this type of activity, identity transformations occur rapidly if the intuitiveness (reading of cues and presentational factors) of the individual does not alert him to something that contradicts expectations. The perspective of the homosexual is one of "open-ended possibilities," as long as he is motivated in beginning the series of significant communications, and encouraged to continue the gestural conversation. Therefore, the social world is transformed into a wide open arena of possible sexual encounters albeit a silent one.

SILENCE IN PUBLIC EROTIC ACTIVITIES: THE MARRIAGE OF SOCIAL FACT AND SEXUAL FANCY

By silence, of course, is meant the absence of verbal exchange and communications. One can attribute the pervasiveness of it to the public nature of the settings in which erotic episodes occur, particularly toilets, parks, beaches, and movie houses. Because other's identity is ambiguous, open verbal solicitation with reference to sexual overtures is dangerous. Speech fixes intentions. Any doubt of another individual's sexual identity necessarily prohibits verbal overtures.

In spaces susceptible to direct coercion and control, silence is used to veil erotic intentions. The public toilet, for example, particularly discourages verbal exchange because any din would draw the attention of the authorities. At the first sound of noise in fact the cubicle empties. It violates the tacitly accepted norms of "doing" toilet sex. The observer vividly recalls one instance that occurred in a subway john in Queens on the IND line.[10] Six people were in the john including the observer. Two men at the urinals, absorbed in staring at each other's penis, massaged full erections for all to see. Both commodes were occupied. One man licked his lips toward the observer as an invitation to fellatio, while the other masturbated and stared at the observer's groin. (The observer had positioned himself opposite the wall upon which the commodes and urinals were placed.) Alongside of the observer stood a blond-haired youth, about 25, who smiled frequently (rarely done in toilets). Having stared at the graffiti that covered the walls, with the usual emphasis on large genitals, the young man turned to the observer and said aloud, "This writing really turns me on!" Everyone stopped what they were doing, quietly looked at the young man, adjusted clothing, and within two minutes departed.

The fact that others surrounding the eroticist are strangers, or that particular settings require silence, does not adequately explain the widespread use of the phenomenon, especially in settings where those present are known to be homosexual — patrons of the gay bar or gay bath, for example. Even though the gay bar is a wonder of noise, a mixture of loud chatter and blasting music, the individual disassociates himself from consociate circles and verbal sociation and enters the arena of silent discourse during erotic maneuvering. The bath, brimming with immediately accessible bodies, is characterized by silence. The intentions of the actors in both settings form a singular erotic frame of reference and yet silent discourse is the only web of communication employed in establishing liaisons. Why?

As a controlling device, silence modifies situational communications and interaction, focusing them on erotic significations (see Goffman, 1959, on information control). Falling somewhere between the signs actually sent and those the recipient thinks or hopes he saw, visualization builds tension and passion in the silent void. The rich and delicate fabric of silent "embodied" information evokes sexual concourse, enhances the credibility and desirability of erotic communicants, and permits easy withdrawal in dangerous situations and those that prove hopelessly frustrating, misdirected, and otherwise erotically wrong (for a general discussion of physical language, see Hall, 1959). When silence shrouds a situation and cues are restricted to present and apparent physical sign vehicles, the "actual" self of the individual is not discoverable (see Goffman, S1963: 2). The "visual" self as presented in the setting is "the" person as far as those present are concerned. Claims to erotic identities take place only through the sign equipment, manners, and decorum of the sexual parameters of the moment and have little relationship to the bundle of attributes and definitions obtained and in use in the larger conventional world. During homosexual moments contiguous to everyday rounds of activity, the erotic vocabulary glosses over contradictory appearances — the guy in a suit, for example, supposedly masculine and "butch," can still fellate someone "logically" by taking a commode seat in a public toilet, which signals his sexual interests.

On the individual level then; the "actual" self as an idiosyncratic combination of biography and role repertoire, remains purposefully obscured. "Virtual" or sexual identity becomes the center of attention and interaction, that is, the erotic typification is the magnet drawing attention.

If biographical elements play little part in erotic presentations, sexual portrayals assume the directorship in liaisons; and these portraits emerge from the sexual fantasies of those who parade them. In settings that foster particular identities, the correct appropriation of "gear" and the adoption of the expected presentation is of maximal importance. The individual who is into "leather," for example, does not have to worry about the debilitating effect his interior decorating job would have on a leather image. He does not have to tell anyone. Leather jacket, hat, trousers, and boots, all preferably black and studded with various metal accessories of stars, chains, and eagles, bestow conviction on his portrayal.

In addition to appropriate "sign vehicles" in silent situations, erotic statements equally depend on convincing posturing (Goffman, S1963: 43–48). The leather patron cannot make a claim to seriousness if he acts "nelly" while in leather "drag."[11] Every visible movement conforms to the expected behavior of a leather number. The most prevalent posture in the leather bar, for example, is the studied stance along the bar, one foot on the footrail that encircles the base of the bar, one hand in the rear trouser pocket, the torso slightly twisted toward the main area of the room, eyes, gazing nowhere, peer under the brim of a leather hat that has been pulled far enough down over the face to create shadows and mystery. Leaning on the opposite wall from the bar, one patron's favorite pose consists of legs crossed at the ankles with his "basket" propped up to suggest an immense penis. Hands, folded at the belt, grasp a beer. The head is tilted toward the floor upon which his gaze seems cemented. An air of indifference is managed at all times, assuring viewers of an inner security in the postured image.

The impersonality of silence helps separate the heterosexual and homosexual spheres of an eroticist's biography. When he enters a setting for sex, the homosexual leaves behind the social self of everyday society and its indices of prestige, status, and moral values. They have no bearing on the erotic system unless they contribute to the imagery of the situation. Likewise, when the person departs from an erotic setting, values of the erotic moment are left behind, easily locked out of consciousness by the suspended involvement buoyed by anonymous silence. The simple shutting of a toilet door, a ride on a ferryboat between "straightsville" and Fire Island, or crossing the street from or to a notorious park serve as "rites of passage" that transform one moral reality into another, evoking an easy passage from the realm of the everyday to that of the sensually sexual (Berger and Luckmann, 1967: 99). Hence, silence effectively compartmentalizes public erotic activities, assuaging anxiety and any would-be guilt while enhancing carnal pleasure.

Although social action is goal oriented, the lack of verbalization makes it seem less so. In the silent face-to-face situation, the participant remains a stranger, albeit a physically intimate one. He is able to focus on sexual activities to a degree that would be much more difficult to do if speech revealed his emotions, ideas, ideals, social status, occupation, group affiliations, and other biographical data. Only a transient landscape of sexual fantasy momentarily but wholly fills social horizons, disappearing with the withdrawal of those who sustain it.

Pursued, encountered, and ended without a word spoken, the anonymity of silent erotic episodes is so complete that the individual has difficulty remembering that he has had sex. John B. of Philadelphia "did" (fellated) 17 numbers in one evening at the baths. When asked what he thought of the people involved, he could not remember them. Even forgetting the details of each sexual transaction, all he recalled was that he did 17 — the number seemingly more important than any of the particulars.

DISRUPTIVE, WOULD-BE PLAYERS: THE FRAGILITY OF SILENT COMMUNITY APPEARANCES

The public eroticist quietly nurtures sexual identity in secret. He carefully harbors it from notoriety. Engaging in public sex, he does so with no intention of contesting discrimination against homosexuality. There is no drive to change existing moral conditions. The homosexual adapts to the contingencies of the existing order of things.[12] He maintains socially prescribed and expected demeanor in the round of settings through which he travels. His dual concern is erotic fun without stigmatization. That is what the whole game is about.

"Patriotic swishes" threaten carefully poised imagery (Goffman, S1963: 114). Overtly gay, they make deviant impressions without regard for where they are, regardless of the social consequences their impressions reap. They disregard situational demeanor and refuse to accept contextual constraints on behavior. Unconcerned with any game orientation, they do not feel restrained by social opprobrium. Their behavior no longer reflects the fear of negative sanctions and possible social abuse. No longer interested in sustaining the separation between conventional and unconventional pursuits, their presence threatens those who wish to engage in secret erotic activities. They destroy the "spontaneous" involvement of normals in the situation by attracting their attention. The patriotic swish's appearance often causes sudden and total disintegration of sexual scenes. For example, a flamboyantly dressed individual swept into a west side IRT subway toilet on a summer afternoon. He was an older man with thinly plucked eyebrows arched over inquisitive blue eyes. A long mane of grey hair hung about a pair of thin shoulders that were covered by an outrageously colored shirt. Strands of gold and silver chain clung about the neck. Reeking with cologne, the tearoom filled with a sweet, tenacious fragrance. Upon entering, he "swished" up to the urinal and began looking about the room. He massaged his penis into an erection with a heavily bejeweled hand, hoping for some response. The five individuals present were spartanly dressed in bluejeans and teeshirts. Much younger than the new entrant, they made signs of disgust as the older man began his cueing. Unabashed by their disgust, he turned from the urinal to expose his erection. The others turned their backs to him. He steadfastly persisted, continuing to masturbate. Within a few minutes, first one and then another of the original group left the tearoom. A few minutes more and the rest followed, leaving the old man alone to amuse himself. Anyone coming into the john during this episode would immediately size up the identity of the old man and by a simple process of extrapolation apply the same label to the others present.

Another category of individual who menaces the population under study is the gay liberationist. Wearing identity pegs of liberation, e.g., lamdha buttons, earrings, and even parts of female drag, he not only does not give a damn like the patriotic swish, but actually hopes to destroy the game orientation of gay "brothers" who are still playing at it. His presence in public settings also destroys most erotic situations for the same reasons that the attendance of the patriotic swish does. He attracts attention and does not conform with the sexual fantasies of those in attendance. If either type of individual is interested in "making out" with game-oriented people, they have to assume expected appearances and roles in the game. The aforementioned Dolly is a good case in point. He sets aside his usual effeminate and swishy drag and behavior before entering public toilets. Many GAA members discard liberation drag to actively join in public erotic work.[13]

HOMOSEXUALITY AND STIGMA: LIFE BECOMES "MANAGEABLE"

Public eroticists eat, sleep, work, and relax like everyone else. And like everyone else, they conform to the daily expectations of a work-a-day world (Gagnon and Simon, 1968: 355). Socially prescribed ways of dressing, behaving, speaking, and presenting oneself as a "masculine" person are followed during daily activities.

Socialized into society's beliefs and values, the homosexual is also made aware of the possibility of stigmatization.[14] As Goffman (S1963:7) succinctly points out, "the standards he has incorporated from the wider society equip him to be intimately alive to what others see as his failing, inevitably causing him, if only for moments, to agree that he does indeed fall short of what he really ought to be." To the degree the homosexual feels his sexual orientation will "spoil" aspects of his identity in one or many of the multitude of social relationships in which he routinely participates, that he may be discredited, and that this discreditability is meaningful to him, relationships with others will be viewed as problematical (Goffman, S1963: 4).

The homosexual's problematical orientation to a situation in which he wishes to withhold information about his sexual identity, or direct it to only a few who may be present, propels him outside spontaneous situational involvement. He becomes an observer, tailoring action in accordance with what he interprets as others' expectations of him in a particular role (Cooley, 1964: 184). Because of the threat of stigmatization, the public eroticist monitors identity and self-presentation to avoid detection. The nonthreatened normal does not share similar anxiety and is not alive to bracketing reality over this concern, although he may be alive to other contingencies that interest him. The disattendance of the normal and the attendance of the homosexual to possible stigmatization contribute to the successful "passing" of the public eroticist in mixed situations and are conducive to the ability to sustain conventional demeanor while engaging in public erotic activity. In order to maintain the status quo and the social stability in relationships with others, he consciously manipulates behavior, imagery, and self-presentations to conform to taken-for-granted ones.

Tensions resident in a problematic status elicit a strong desire to create social distance between spheres of licit and illicit behavior by separating possibly confounding audiences. The strategies in generating sexual encounters include the selection of sites in the schedule of daily activities that maximizes social distance between him and his conventional world (Sumner, 1906).

Heightened aliveness to a situation aids the homosexual in not only managing secret information about himself, but also sensitizes his perception in the discernment of erotic amusement and the degree of risk in pursuing it. Continuously bracketing everyday reality, each step in a day's routine becomes part of a vast erotic panorama.[15] The subway, for example, is a dull necessity in the normal's work-a-day routine but can be an eventful, thrilling experience for the public eroticist. Some city subway cars (now out of service) were particularly conducive to sexual activity. Small antechambers flanked each end of the car. Men crowded into these small areas, groping and bumping each other, and actually enjoying open sexual contact. Tom M., for example, had an orgasm one morning on his way to work in one such antechamber. Standing next to a conservatively dressed man, the guy opened Tom's trousers without much forewarning and grabbed his penis. Tom's embarrassment and inner tension produced an immediate ejaculation.

NOTES

1. See Jacqueline Scherer (1972: 122-123) for the sense in which the migrant public lovers of this ethnography form a "community" of interest.
2. The observer followed the "follower" of the unsuspecting followed to the latter's apparent home one summer evening (1970) after a heavy petting scene was observed on a crowded, steamy subway car. The outward indices of the house indicated a middle income family. The various toy accessories in the yard suggested one or two children around the ages of six and seven. The "follower" rang the doorbell of the front door after the "followed" had disappeared therein. A young woman answered the door. A few words were exchanged, and the "follower" departed for an unknown destination. The observer assumes this concluded the affair.
3. Dolly was introduced to the observer during the summer of 1968. The latter had asked a gay friend to arrange a group interview with friends who participated in the john scene and would consent to talk about it.
4. A "meat rack" is a designated physical area set off by various boundary devices and obstacles where an individual's physicality can be approached and touched with little forewarning. One's presence is a conscious but unspoken invitation to be "violated." With little ceremony, A can approach B, take out his penis and commence fellating him if B permits. B can either accept the action or openly reject A with an equal lack of ceremony.
5. The actors in this monograph are all conscious risk-takers. They

weigh existential circumstances before making any decision to act out erotically. For a discussion of risk-taking, see Edwin Lemert (1967: 11-12).

6. The population falls under the "crime without victim" category of deviance. They differ from any general definition of homosexual in the sense that their public acts are a direct claim not only against conventional sexual orientations but a host of moral conventions that prohibit sexual encounters in public. The "victims" in public moments are not, at least initially, the mutual participants, but those who happen to either stumble on the activity or suddenly perceive what they were unaware of, and whose moral sensibilities ar shocked and outraged. The public eroticist then becomes the "victim" when apprehended by the police, or physically abused by social others due to a misplacement of erotic interest. See Edwin Shur (1965).

7. Goffman, B1963, refers to *Behavior in Public Places,* and Goffman, S1963, refers to *Stigma.*

8. Homosexuals are "on the make" when actively prosecuting sexual ends.

9. "Trade" is a very specific type of sexual relationship in homosexual circles. The "trade" individual does not reciprocate in the sexual exchange. He brings a penis and usually an orgasm to the transaction. The "homosexual" is the active participant, eliciting the trade's orgasms by performing fellatio or accepting anal sodomy. The relationship is a psychologically complex one. The trade member is theoretically defined as highly masculine ("butch") while the homosexual partner is merely something else — but not masculine. That the entire transaction is maintained with "tongue-in-cheek" is captured by the cynical quip: "Today's trade is tomorrow's competition."

10. Actual names of erotic settings already well known in the media or no longer in existence are used in the study. The names of little known and active settings are substituted with a dash or abbreviation.

11. "Drag" in gay circles referred at one time mainly to female attire and the active attempt in staging a convincing "female" impression. Pete Fisher, author of *The Gay Mystique: The Myth and Reality of Male Homosexuality* (1971), clarified the word's meaning during a general membership meeting at the Gay Activist Alliance. Pete and his lover, Marc, always appeared in leather during these meetings. He stated that they were wearing drag. He stated that all attire is drag. It is worn purposely to effect an impression. The businessman has a business drag — suit, tie, and wing-tipped shoes. Rather than confining drag to female costuming, he expanded the definition to include the active concern of everyone in maintaining certain imagery through attire. Fisher's statement on drag is the accepted one used in this study.

12. The covert homosexual is an "aberrant" deviant — dedicated to the quest of erotic activities within the system rather than changing the rules of society as the nonconformist (e.g., the gay activist) would. He does so, as explained below, because he has vested, erotic interests

in the existing status quo (see Merton, 1971: 830).

13. GAA is the abbreviation of the Gay Activist Alliance, a once vociferous, now mostly dormant gay activist organization. The observer attended organizational functions over a three-year period while doing research.

14. For a comprehensive listing of what these negative reactions could be, see Humphreys, 1972: Chapter 2.

15. The homosexual is definitely "other-directed." See Reisman, 1950.

chapter 2

Public Spaces as Erotic Arenas

ACCESSIBILITY

Public is defined as "any region in a community freely accessible to members of that community" (Goffman, B1963: 9). No physical or social obstacles prevent attendance. Freedom of access is taken for granted. Streets, parks, and retail stores for example are open to all.

However, settings are associated with certain images, expectations, and appropriate behavior that modify accessibility (Lyman and Scott, 1970: 91). Differences reside in the common sense appropriation and utilization of the setting by various social groups. These differences contribute to the separation of erotic and non-erotic populations. Returning to the example of the park, the community in general enjoys

the green environs during the day. At night, few groups dare to enter. Homosexuals, muggers, an occasional strolling heterosexual couple, or undercover agents are the exceptional visitors.

Furthermore, the routine of an individual's everyday activities fix populations and hence erotic types in certain territories. The Canal Street subway toilet, for example, is heavily used by working-class people of various ethnic groups during the work week. Upper east side IRT subway toilets, reflecting the neighborhoods above the ground, tend to be rather homogeneously white, middle class, and white-collar. Gay bars located in the isolated extreme West Village beacon to "western" and "S-M" oriented identities.[2] Subway toilets situated in West Village stations attract the same types. Those who find these categories of individuals of sexual interest will also be drawn to them.

Two general types of public settings arrogated by the homosexual for erotic activity can be distinguished by virtue of their accessibility. "Natural theaters of action" refer to settings usurped by public eroticists but not intended for this purpose. Totally accessible to the general public, given the preceding qualifications, they are in no way intended for sexual activities. Because of ecological factors, however, the settings facilitate sexual activity. Two universal natural theaters, at least in the occident, are the park and public toilet.

The second type of public erotic setting is the subcultural one that specifically encourages erotic posturing if not outright sex. Privately owned, they are not nearly as accessible to the public as natural settings. The homosexual bar and bath are prime examples.

The openness of homosexual identity statements very inversely with the publicness of the setting. Communications are highly ambiguous on the street and in the tearoom where information about those in copresence is difficult to ascertain, but rather direct in the gay bar and bath whose population is presumed to be homogeneously homosexual.

Familiar grids of action, especially those that have acquired a reputation for successful sexual activity, aid the interested homosexual in the adroit placement of erotic pursuits in public. The "trucks" and certain subway toilets in which successful erotic encounters have taken place create a sense of security.[3] Familiarity, however, does not mean safety. Even in well-known settings where identities are assumed to be "ecologically fixed," the knowledge one has of those about him is rather hypothetical. If another individual responds in a seemingly reciprocal way, the interested party assumes that both are sharing a mutual frame of reference. But this is the danger. Such moments are generated on tenuous cues, communications, and assumptions at best. Who the eroticist "really" is, is always conjectural, paradoxically representing gratification and danger, hope and fear. Due to their public and topical nature, the processes of recognition must be subtle.[4] The necessary subtlety reinforces the possibility and and danger of misplaced endeavor. The several "S-M" men who took someone home from one of the Village leather bars — a place of safety — and were subsequently murdered no doubt assumed the murderer to be one of them.[5]

VISIBILITY

The possibility of the presence of an audience, even if none exists, creates visibility, or the sense of it during public encounters. Audiences, of course, are desired. Fellow eroticists and other individuals who vicariously participate in and help sustain the illicit moment are drawn from their midsts. Public avenues to sexual ends, after all, supply a wide selection of public settings in which to participate and attract an unlimited population of homosexual others from which to draw.

The visibility or observability that the out-in-the-open quality of public activity portends varies with the accessibility of the setting and with those who are actually or suspected of being present. Erotic statements vary considerably with different degrees of visibility, e.g., covert identity statements on the street but flagrant ones in sequestered areas that are accompanied by extreme sub-cultural dress and mannerisms.

By the obverse, visibility threatens dramatic self-disclosure. Public and semi-public gathering places are subject to coercion by agents of control. Although 11 states have legalized private homosexual activity between consenting adults, all states censure public erotic acts, both homosexual and heterosexual, and any public behavior that leads to either public or private sexual acts (*The Advocate,* 1975: 4). Even in states that permit homosexual activity in private between consenting adults, legal proscriptions exists against "lewd and lascivious acts," indecent exposure, and loitering, under which public homosexual erotic behavior is usually prosecuted.[6] Public and private homosexual activity in New York City, the area of the study, is proscribed by the New York State Revised Penal Code of 1965 (Marks and Papnerno, 1967).

Whether actively enforced or not, fear of apprehension, personal abuse, and the possible social affects they have on one's biography create a threat to the homosexual who engages in public eroticism. These fears extend to the semi-institutionalized settings of the gay bar and gay bath, which may be attended by impostors as noted above.[7] In another instance, "Baskett was arrested April 3, near Lucy's at the corner of Broadway and Orange in Long Beach, where he admitted offering a ride to a man who turned out to be a vice officer" (*The Advocate,* 1971: 11). The vice officer had been seen previously that evening at Lucy's (gay bar) by the arrested subject. Entrapment of this kind poses very serious problems for the public eroticist. Illegitimate claims, identities, and communications are not only known and utilized by vice agents but played out with great authenticity for the purposes of making successful arrests. The dilemma and ambiguity between gratifying and threatening elements haunt the homosexual during public forays.

Erratic enforcement of the law does not reduce fear of apprehension. It merely creates instability in erotic placement, and necessitates greater risk-taking. Frequenting public settings not widely known for homosexual activities is encouraged, and better known settings are avoided because they are assumed to threaten more immediate legal sanctions or self-disclosure. The logic for the behavior rests on the assumption that, if homosexual others can be identified in settings other than "known" gay spots, erotic activity can proceed on a relatively safe basis. Successful interruption by the police or vice squad seem less apt to happen.

The utilitarian purposes of public spaces aid in the reduction of visibility during sexual activity and curb the chances of apprehension. If the homosexual brackets everyday routine to discern erotic others and sexual possibilities, the normal is spontaneously involved with the utilitarian motif of the setting, or "alive" to a different set of contingencies that interest him or her (boy looking for a receptive girl, and vice versa). Shoulder to shoulder, side by side, and looking "past" the clandestine activities of the other, different categories of the urban mass assume that his neighbor will honor the commonly shared and morally defined definitions of public demeanor and behavior, in spite of private interests (Goffman, B1963). In effect, multiple social realities can be manipulated in the same time and space zone as long as the knowledge of one can somehow be safeguarded from the other (Schutz, 1967).

Lastly, many public places do provide some sort of obstacles that interfere with visibility and veil unconventional activity. A bar called Beau Brummel located in the east 50s in Manhattan during the early 1960s is an excellent example. According to Bob C., a space salesman and frequent attender, the bar catered to a rather wealthy homosexual clientele during the lunch and early afternoon hours. Management deflected any heterosexual attendance. Light cruising and some quiet petting took place among patrons. Promptly at 7:00 p.m. bartenders changed. With this cue, the gay crowd dispersed and the straight one arrived. Management then reversed its filtering processes. The observer witnessed the same phenomenon in Quebec City, but in a reverse time sequel. At 10:00 p.m. the Alouette changed from a very heavy, stodgy businessman's restaurant into a wild dancing gay club. A toilet without a door will house very little erotic activity compared to one with a coin-lock. Access to the former is too easy and very dangerous for erotic use. A well-lit park with minimal shrubbery hosts little erotic activity in contrast to a dark, well-planted one. Facades, doors, and other obstacles that create time zones of forewarning against surprise entrants create boundaries, separating various audiences, expectations and behavior, and provide recovery time during moments of interruption.

IDENTIFYING HOMOSEXUAL OTHERS IN PUBLIC CONTEXTS

The analysis of public settings has been arranged into a continuum of closed, or slightly suspicious contexts to entirely open ones depending on the degree of certainty one has of the other's homosexual identity (Glaser and Strauss, 1967: 429-444). They are presented in this sequence because some situational factors contributing to identification are not as apparent in one context as they are in another. But all, directly or indirectly, contribute to erotic identification in each setting. For example, closed contexts, such as the street, raise the fundamental problem of recognizing a fellow homosexual in circumstances devoid of identity information. There is a poverty of attendant cues. Mobilizing self into erotic interest, surmounting everyday engrossment, attending to a singular individual who may be part of a large aggregate, focusing in on him with erotic intentions, and above all, communicating this interest in such a way that it can be disavowed if misdirected while, at the same time, helping the individual transform his absorption in everyday concerns into erotic ones, are some of the complexities in a spontaneous, closed awareness context.

In contrast to the spontaneous context, open contexts preclude the foregoing as specific problems. Gay bar or bath attendance presumes a population of interested, erotically motivated homosexual patrons.[8] In these settings, other matters come to the fore. Establishing and managing correct identity, given a setting's sexual reputation, and securing a firm place on the continuum of desirability are only two of many concerns absent from a closed context (because erotic interest must have been mobilized in the spontaneous encounter for it to occur, imagery and desirability can be of no concern by definition). Open contexts assure the presence of erotic others but do not guarantee contact. Given spatial contingencies and the facts known about or read into them, attendance in a public setting will be a firm, suspicious, questionable or unknown identity statement of the self. The type of awareness in various public settings determine the ease with which erotic identities can be avowed, and the concomitant probability of a successful contact. It has strong if tacit implications for communications and interaction, being instrumental in situating erotic events (Stone, 1962).

NOTES

1. See Robert Ardrey, 1966: 42-80, for a discussion of arena behavior in the animal kingdom. The public eroticist utilizes posturing and gestural stimuli seemingly similar to that employed by the animal world during courting rituals.

2. "Western" types are individuals who effect rugged, masculine behavior and emphasize this self-conception by wearing denim trousers, plaid shirts, boots, heavy belts, and an occasional cowboy hat. Currently (1973), the image also includes beard, mustache, or any combination of either. "S-M" refers to superordinate-subordinate sexual identities and roles. Self-presentations are usually made in leather or suede, with an elaborate system of indices that distinguish one from the other. For example, keys worn on the left belt loop of the trousers rather than the right one indicates an "S" identity. The reverse placement signifies an "M." The roles are mutually complementary (and supportive). Subtle cueing is crucial for compatibility and the prevention of role embarrassment. For a succinct, well-written and interesting description of S-M, see Richard Goldstein, 1975: 10-13.

3. The "trucks" referred to in this study are parked near docks under the West Side Highway. During the day, they are loaded with merchandise

and freight unloaded from arriving ships. At night and parked empty, the rear of the truck is left open. No one seems to guard them during the long evening hours of darkness except for an occasional patrol by the city police. Public eroticists climb aboard and participate in continual orgies from 10:00 p.m. to 4:00 a.m. The urban location of the parked trucks is empty, dark, and gloomily silent.

The trucks have shifted twice in location. The first change occurred when a foot of Christopher Street was transformed from a parking lot into a riverside park. The second dislocation took place in response to the construction of new housing. During the past two decades, and in spite of relocations, they have facilitated an enormous amount of public sexuality and have acquired a large congregation of devoted followers. It is common practice of the Eagle, Spike, and Keller crowds (all leather bars) to empty at closing time and head for the trucks for sex. Ending many hours of drinking and posturing the rigid identities of leather — a visual contest of presenting competing claims to "authentic" leather identities — individuals head for the trucks, where darkness smothers all identities except for the anatomical ones.

Although the observer has been around the peripheries of the trucks many times, he has been inside only once, and that visit was very brief. No role existed for him in the soundless murkiness that would create social distance between himself and erotic others. Dr. E. and Dr. P. have been the observer's main source of information. A similar problem existed for Ponte (1974) when he tried observing homosexual transactions via cars. He was isolated in his own vehicle. Because he did not wish to engage in erotic dialogues to collect data, he was shut out from the nexus of events that culminated in either a pick-up or rejection between communicants.

4. "Marginal people become sensitive to marginal cues, any measure of freedom they obtain being dependent upon quick appraisal of the intentions, moods and messages of others" (Humphreys, 1972: 67).

5. Fear gripped the homosexual community in Greenwich Village's leather scene when it was reported in *The New York Times*, January 18, 1973, that three violent murders were discovered involving patrons of leather bars. The separate incidences, all very similar to each other, raised the ugly spectre that someone who knew the game was "fishing" out victims from local leather bars.

6. See West, 1967: Chapter IV, for an international review of legal proscriptions against homosexuality and related activities.

7. One example is the raid by the Suffolk Police on the Corral Bar in Holbrock, New York. See *Gay*, 1972.

8. In New York City prior to Lindsay' election in 1965, entrapment could take place in any public context, taking the problem of "recognition" into the "safest" settings. Weinberg and Williams (1974: 33-34) describe a police raid on the Continental Baths on February 20, 1969. After a policeman entered the baths "as a homosexual" and observed what was going on, he called in a raid. Twenty-two arrests were made.

chapter 3

Sex in Pedestrian Places

The Spontaneous Encounter

INTUITIVE INSIGHTS INTO HIDDEN IDENTITIES

Chiefly characterized by a lack of erotic intentions on the actor's part, surprise in recognizing a fellow eroticist, and a paucity of identity information supporting erotic claims, beliefs, and possible sexual interaction, the spontaenous encounter blossoms in "unfocused" areas of everyday routine (see Merton, 1949, Chapter II, for a discussion of "serendipity"). They take place in the terribly pedestrian places of social life — on mass transportation, the street, and other conduits that form links between one social enterprise and another. They explode out of the mundane, "unfateful" rounds of commonplace activities (for a discussion of "fatefulness," see Goffman, 1967: 161-170).

By definition, recognition transpires in areas not pre-defined as conducive to homosexual activity. Self-impressions are geared for other-than-erotic contexts, and not for self-disclosure in the pursuit of homosexual goals. The "surprise" of the encounter is precipitad by the sudden "intuitive" recognition that someone in copresence is no longer regarded with civil inattention but becomes the focus of erotic attention. How is everyday engrossment transcended by the homosexual in the recognition of an individual he suspects of being another homosexual? Dropping subtle cues and clues will not mobilize attention because both individuals are engrossed in the routine of their daily preoccupations and will not notice them.

Homosexuals are erotically attracted to sexual objects of the same sex. Every male however is not sexually interesting and deserving of attention. "Types" of sexual objects signifying maximum erotic interest are carried in the eddies of fancy in the mental make-up of the homosexual, which now and again intrude on his stream of consciousness. The appearance of a "type" on the horizon of the individual mobilizes attention along erotic lines, suspending, even if momentarily, socio-spatial engrossment.

"Types" refer to a congelation of physical, behavioral, self-presentational, and social characteristics that are symbolically significant to the homosexual's erotic interest, pursuits, and gratification. Idiosyncratic to each individual, they form a continuum of most to least interesting, and attract or deflect attention accordingly. Any male that conforms to the symbolic constellation of an erotic type agitates attention of the public eroticist. Interest is evoked regardles of location. Dr. P., an eye surgeon, for example, gets "turned on" by middle-aged men of good build. During a routine eye examination of a patient who conformed to Dr. P's type, the latter was unable to maintain emotional neutrality. Only his smock covered a growing sexual arousal.[2]

"Types" of "types" are inexhaustibly diverse. Individuals prefer, for example, only white or black men, or both, given other criteria; fat or slim men; muscular men only; blond, black, or red-headed men; bald men; short, medium, or tall men; men who are white-collar, blue-collar, or wealthy; and any combination of these and many, many other qualities. By way of illustration, the individual who has a trim, firm body, is white, dresses in jeans or leather, and conforms to his sexual practices (S-M) maximally excites Dr. E. Dr. E will not reciprocate fellatio with anyone having a small penis so that, once undressed, the sexual type must have a large penis. A large penis will compensate for color and inadequate physique to some extent. Accompanying Dr. E on a walk confirms the fact the he only sees a small range of the number of men on the street, all of whom usually conform to his type.

Middle class men seize the erotic attention of Mr. V. To enlist his interest, they must look prosperous. Suit and tie, and a slight overweight physique elicit his interest. Mr. X of Brooklyn Heights, a short, well-muscled individual searches only for the obese. Men of sagging corpulence stimulate acute interest. A middle-aged Swedish man confesses that blacks alone provoke sexual arousal. A Brooklyn Jew repeats the same assertion.

Some public eroticists need a setting to arouse sexual interest. Only individuals within a setting, given additional criteria, elicit interest. Peter bends and twists everyday rounds of activity around the route of his favorite toilets because sex to him means sex in toilets. For such individuals, spontaneous encounters are not possible.

LATENT EVIDENCE OF THE PRESENCE
OF SILENT COMMUNICANTS

Another element in mobilizing erotic interest is the belief that the individual drawing attention really might be a fellow homosexual. These belief "frames" are amorphous but highly crucial for the evolvement of an encounter. If we compare some of these frames in different geographic areas, the slender threads of evidence that advance sexual episodes discreetly surface. In the empirical street scene sketched below, the chance encounter takes place in a section of town reputed to have a dense homosexual population. Retail stores are cruisy, particularly one department store renowned for its elegance. The area's reputation lends credence to the belief that any male on the street or within the area may be a homosexual and receptive to erotic overtures. A mutual exchange of interest between two men in such an area creates an "intuitive" belief that the other is a likely candidate for erotic discourse and confirms the credibility of the likelihood of a venture.

Compare this to John R's sexual encounter in an isolated motel bar in a very small town in New Mexico.[3] Alone with one other male patron who sported a wedding ring on his finger (an implicit credential of heterosexuality — at least on first reading), the last thing in John's mind was "making out." The possibility that the other man was homosexual given the remoteness of the setting seemed so ludicrous that the thought never entered consciousness. The two men drifted together through conversation, discussing the weather, work, travels, family, and present surroundings. Because neither was tired as closing time approached, John purchased a bottle of booze, and both retired to the other patron's room. The isolation of the motel, the "one chance in a million" that the patron was a homosexual, and the glaring evidence of the wedding ring precluded any suspicion on John's part that the man was anything other than heterosexual. As both men became inebriated, conversation broached sexual topics and John's leg was touched. John R was overwhelmingly surprised. The professionalism of the patron's sexual participation, according to John, indicated that the man was no novice to homosexual activity.

In short, the unnoticed, supportive background relevance structures play a very important part in mobilizing suspicion in even the least structured setting (Garfinkel, 1967: Chapter II). However, even in densely populated areas that seem to be populated by large numbers of homosexuals, encounters between various categories of people who are suspicious of each other rarely occur. Recognition depends on credibility, which in turn begets social trust. Interracial contacts on the street are minimal, for example, because racial prejudice interferes with establishing social trust. The motivations of the individual remain suspect. Yet, the same two males can close the gap in trust with some measure of assurance in a public toilet, and most certainly in a gay bath or gay bar.

Only in the spontaneous moment do intuitive insights and latent evidence of sexual others play an important part in negotiating an encounter. Other types of situations, analyzed below, are predefined as homosexual or at least homosexually workable. Confined to specific spaces and times in urban routine, they are thought to accommodate sexual activity without the handicap of so much doubt.

A STREET SCENE[4]

As veins and arteries of commerce and leisure, and as conduits to different social enterprises, the street is often traveled with little thought.[5] The purposes and goals of the next stop often preoccupy the pedestrian, as do reassessments of memories of the past, preempting any attention to passing street phenomena. The routine of coming and going commands little if any notice. The individual, dressed according to existing conventional codes exhibits no indication of any hidden identity. Spontaneously involved in the journey to his next destination, he is not consciously looking for an erotic incident. Erotic moments, however, arise in these vacuous, not entirely empty, travels.

East 57th Street horizontally cuts across the island of Manhattan. The street, or that part of it on which the observation was made, is populated with old established furniture and antique shops, and newer bank and office buildings. The traffic on the street is essentially commercial, comprised mostly of well-dressed office workers and an army of messengers and couriers. The observation occurred between noon and 1:00 p.m., lunch time, near one of the major intersections of the street.

The observer was standing idly in front of a window of

quality antiques, watching the reflection of the crowded criss-cross currents of pedestrians. A young man in his early 20s emerged from out of one of the four commercial banks that garrison the corners of the intersection. Dressed in a suit and topcoat — nothing out of the ordinary — he was swept into the hurrying throng. Once in the crowd, he walked in the observer's direction, assuming the pedestrian "blank look." Approximately five yards from the observer, the attitude of the young man suddenly altered. His eyes fixed on something. They stared with steady intensity. The observer followed the direction of the young man's gaze. About 20 yards east of the observer, a man in his late 30s or early 40s was walking in his direction. He seemed oblivious to all around him. He too wore a suit and topcoat in the chilly, grey weather. The approaching individual seemed unaware of the commanding interest he inspired in the young man. Abruptly, with only ten feet distance between them, the older man's focused on the young man's face and both held a prolonged stare until each walked past the other (slightly to the right of the observer). The gait of each slowed. When they reached about five yards from each other, first the one and then the other stopped, turned and once again exchanged brief but intense stares. At this time, the observer vacated his position in front of the show window and moved up the street.

The young man changed the direction of his travels and walked over to the show window, occasionally looking back over his shoulder in the direction of the other man. He stood in front of the show window, peering in at the splendidly displayed antiques. The other man, hereafter known as Mr. X, altered his course of travel and slowly moved to the same window. He assumed a position of about five feet from Mr. Z, and also looked at the furniture. Hard stares continued to pass between them, aided by the reflection of the glass window — but no speech. Mr. Z gradually pulled away from the window, and resumed walking in the same direction he had been going before the encounter. He repeatedly looked back at Mr. X. Mr. X hesitantly changed the course of his walk, and followed Mr. Z. The two men continued in this

direction, carefully maintaining a ten-foot distance between them, Mr. X in back and to the side of Mr. Z. When
they reached the building on the corner, they separately
hurried into it. (The observer kept pace with them, unnoticed in the sidewalk multitude.)

The corner building that Messrs. X and Z entered is a
residential hotel for women. An old established gay bar
occupies part of the lobby floor and is known for its lunch
clientele (the bar is dull during evening hours). Also on the
lobby floor and not connected with the bar is an entrance to
a public toilet for men through which Mr. X and Mr. Z disappeared. (The toilet was closed after the lobby floor was re-
modeled a year after the observation was made.) The toilet
had a well-known public erotic reputation.

Although the observer did not verbally communicate with
the interactants, it was apparent that both men were
strangers to each other (recognition without verbal sal-
utations). Of course, either may have seen the other in
another gay setting but both were strangers to each other.
Why else maintain street decorum without speaking while
standing in front of the show window? The encounter
certainly was spontaneous: the suddenness of perception,
the ambiguity in the carefully maintained distance while
standing in front of the shop window, and the fact that both
were dressed for a white-collar routine rather than a
"cruising one."

THE INITIAL IDENTITY PROBE

The most pervasive opening probe into suspect persons
regardless of location is the initial glance. Initial eye
contact is not merely an empty glance but a holding or
penetrating look shot directly into other's eyes. The piercing
look is a visual inquiry into the possible homosexual identity
of the other, simultaneously making an initial statement of
the sender's interest in him. It is the first "direct" step
toward the possible transformation of the moment into an
erotic one. If reciprocated in the intensity considered

necessary, eye contact initiates recognition, at least fleetingly. If there is no response, the eroticist simply resumes suspended preoccupations.

The searching, questioning glance can be withdrawn immediately, recovering the slight, other-than-normal interest without undue notice, assuring others present who may have witnessed the unusual look that what they thought they saw was misinterpreted by them. The ease of withdrawal is terribly important during moments of initial thrusts because the threat of embarrassment is always present.[6] The hardness of the stare can be softened if reciprocity is not forthcoming.

No commitment resides in this type of glance except for those who can read the intended message. However, as Goffman (B1963: 95) points out, "mutual glances ordinarily must be withheld if an encounter is to be avoided, for eye contact opens one up for face engagement."

That there is something in these searching looks is apparent from the reactions they elicit. The erotic "glance" may be brief, but intense. The recipient of them becomes alert to the fact that he is being stared at. Walking on the street with Frankie F. one late afternoon, for example, the observer noticed Frankie looking very hard at a group of young men approaching from the opposite direction. Frankie stared at one individual at great length. The latter automatically felt his zipper, and followed it with a visual self-appraisal to make sure he was not exposed.

CONFIRMATORY GESTURES

Eye contact is a good indication of but not sufficient evidence for homosexual identity statements. Additional cues are necessary to convert suspicion into belief. Confirming moves in conventional contexts conform to everyday protocol and demeanor. On the street, for example, interested strangers follow brief searching looks with longer-held stares as each passes the other. Then both stop walking, casually turn, and stare after each other. The "turn around" solidifies evidence of interest, and transforms a suspicious identity into a defined one. In subways, it is only natural to hold onto a supporting pole during the ride, and equally natural to have one's tense hand relax and slip down the pole. That it touches a co-rider's could be ascribed to accident. In the public eroticist's case, however, it is entirely intentional and often employed as a confirming ploy. Identity verification takes place when the opposite hand is not withdrawn but maintains a firm opposing pressure. Bumping the interesting party during the frequent twists and turns of a subway ride is also another favorite confirming technique.[7] If the rider does not move out of the way of the touching body he has indicated a willingness to be touched.

As the eroticist becomes more certain of the homosexuality of the recipient of his advances aspects of conventional demeanor take on erotic qualities. Eyes become recast into significant avenues of the sensual. As agitation deepens, the eyes reflect it, expanding excitement. The way one hangs on a subway strap, or crosses the legs are translated into indicators of a hypothetical sexual identity and attractiveness. Conventional appearance is transmuted into erotic representation.

ESCALATING STRATEGIES

The necessary paucity of escalation equipment in spontaneous encounters focuses the creation of the erotic dialogue on the full presence of the interactants and the communication between them (always circumscribed by the existing social context). Even though communications are visual (and visible to surrounding others), they must intensify if the situation is to emerge as a definite erotic situation. Erections, heavy breathing, various auto-petting gestures, and more graphic body movements accompany hard, holding stares. In areas that permit subtle body contact, such as the crowded subway car, hands or legs search out counterparts and press together, at first fleetingly, and then with some intensity.

Escalating maneuvers must continue if the situation is to be sustained. A suspension of them without apparent reason is interpreted as a loss of interest, prompting situation dissolution. In spite of escalating strategies, spontaneous moments are intrinsically frustrating. Because of the conventionality of the containing "host" setting, they usually do not culminate in physical, orgasmic conclusion. Escalation can be carried only so far when it is realized that to go any further would be dangerous or monotonous. Even though erections routinely bulge through trousers, rarely does overt massaging take place except in crowded settings. In one case, however, the penis was actually pulled out of the trousers and fellated to orgasm behind a staircase on a subway platform during early evening hours (an anecdotal account — June, 1970).

Commuting: An Example of Sexual Escalation in Pedestrian Places

The erotic moment described below occurred during the morning rush hour. For some reason, the arriving train was not as crowded as usual. Bodily contact among fellow passengers was not necessary. When the train pulled into the station, the observer and several men and women of various ages and attired without exception in white-collar drag boarded the car. Two males, in their late 20s, acquired standing positions around one of the central poles in the aisle that flank each end of the car and faced each other. The observer had noted these individuals on the platform as possible eroticists along with several other men. At that time, located some ten yards from each other, they exhibited no apparent interest in one another.

The hand of one man held onto the pole several inches above the other man's grasp. Each had folded his newspaper and tucked it away. They assumed the detached look of the commuting passenger, staring now at advertising posters, now at the people around them, but mostly at nothing. The observer stood against the door facing the pole and also assumed the noninvolved commuter poise.[8]

The two men began (or resumed?) exchanges of brief eye contact, always careful to sustain the commuter poise. Fellow passengers seemed oblivious to the increasingly engrossing dialogue, apparently too absorbed in books, papers, somnolence, or sheer idleness to notice. Before the train reached the next stop, the hands grasping the pole had attained the touch of their counterpart.

When the train stopped at the next station, the crush of boarders forced the observer into the center of the unfolding drama. Forced to change positions somewhat, the actors continued to grasp the pole. As a result of the crowding, Messrs. A and B were shoulder to shoulder, body to body. Mr. A's arm with which he grasped the pole was quite extended. That of Mr. B's formed an acute angle. Due to the reshuffle, they lost visual contact. However, their bodies were so close that the slightest sway of the train swung them together. Indeed, the observer was able to note that not only did their legs remain engaged, but the free hand of each managed to find the groin of the other, engaging in some heavy petting. This took place, it must be remembered, in a crowded subway car with fellow passengers mashed up against them.

When the train pulled into X station, Mr. A debarked from the train. Fleeting, trailing glances passed between A and B as the train pulled out. Once the doors shut and A was gone, B resumed the commuter poise.

While the above exchange took place, a reading of those surrounding the pair indicated that no one seemed aware of what was transpiring. Immersed in newspapers, quiet dozing, and sheer emptiness, and struggling to maintain balance in the conjested, lurching train, fellow passengers seemed so self-involved that their reverie served as an effective blocking device in perceiving the encounter.

BOUNDARIES AND TERMINATION OF SPONTANEOUS EPISODES

Individuals have a sensibility of appropriate and inappropriate behavior in the sundry social situations in which they participate. The line, often hazy, that divides the norm (moral) from the abnormal (immoral) depends on the reciprocal interpretations of the immediate participants and the social others who in some way contribute to the situation as reference others, vicarious participants, or as witnessing nonparticipants, all of whom, by degrees, influence the content of the situation. Because the spontaneous encounter is a situation within a situation, an inextricable enclave within the conventional host setting, deference to the latitudes and constraints of everyday protocol unswervingly continue if social embarrassment is to be prevented. Erotic recognition, signals, and activity proceed divisively; one eye looks to the moral requirements of the conventional context, the other to erotic tactics. For example, the observer was milling about the men's sweater department of a large department store for the purpose of gathering data. He noticed a man, in his early 30s, dressed in a form-fitting checkered shirt, bluejeans, and a long overcoat, seriously glancing his way several times. The observer overlooked the overtures, busying himself with the merchandise.

The man, Mr. O, continued shopping in and around the sweaters, shirts and ties. He began looking at regular intervals toward an individual examining shirts some aisles away.

The object of Mr. O's attention, a man about the same age, was dressed in bluejeans, solid colored shirt, and a short jacket. The observer tuned into the unfolding dialogue as Mr. P became aware of the visual attention of Mr. O. Two parallel counters of shirts separated the two men. They busied themselves about the shirts with intermittent stares passing between them. These brief glances gradually hardened into longer stares. Neither made a move, however, to close the distance separating them.

Visual communication stimulated sexual excitation. Erections developed, and both individuals eyed the arousal of the other (Mr. O's overcoat had been open throughout the period of observation). Ocular discourse grew quite intense. The individuals narrowed the gap that separated them by moving to the opposite sides of a single shirt counter. While doing so they carefully sustained the role of the shopper examining merchandise. The encounter suddenly concluded when Mr P withdrew from the counter and joined a friend who seemed to be waiting for him.

Spun out of the necessities of precaution and safety imposed by conventional imperatives, the delicate, tenuous fabric of the spontaneous moment threads a sense of "boundedness" around participants. Momentary, threatening, and out of place, the spontaneity of the meeting exaggerates the graphicity and immediacy of the encounter, producing a confined, concentrated, and ambiguous sense of emotional tautness. Because meetings take place between rounds of everyday life that ineluctably reimpose their priorities, the episode cannot be drawn out longer, or transported to a new location. When the subway train stops at the passenger's destination, for example, he must debark if he is not to be late for work.

On the other hand, an encounter collapses when one or all of the interactants suspect or perceive "knowledgeable" eyes looking at them, indicating that the boundary between conventional context and erotic scenario has been breached. One subway adventure, for example, abruptly dissolved during escalating maneuvers. The pair had been groping each other's groin when one member unexpectedly broke from the activity and awkwardly retrieved his hand. His face flushed with color. The observer looked around and noted that within a few feet of the couple sat an elderly man taking in the whole drama. The man's face was expressionless but his steady gaze obviated an interest in the couple's unusual activity.[9] The fact that the transaction was witnessed proved too much for the participants. They debarked in opposite directions at the train's next stop.

It does not matter whether the witness is heterosexual or homosexual. If the moral membrane of the conventional context has been penetrated, the rules of the game are compromised, prematurely destroying the episode. Clandestine participation frames the tension-producing spectacle; discovery shatters the scenario. In another instance, the observer boarded a subway car after spending a day observing a gay beach. He sat down on a row of seats beyond an aisle that separated a set of opposite-facing rows. Two men were already seated, facing each other. The observer recognized them as sunbathers from the beach. It was obvious that they were engaged in a heavy visual dialogue. Hard engrossing stares punctuated the passage of every few seconds. A gradually developed an erection that actually dropped out of the shorts he was wearing. He made no attempt to recover the exposure, allowing B to visually dwell on it, even though the subway car was slowly filling with passengers. None of the other passengers seemed to be aware of the situation. Only when another homosexual sat down near B (recognized from the beach) and displayed an awareness and keen interest in the proceedings did A recover the exposed erection. At that moment, B relocated to the next car and A returned to newspaper reading.

An encounter concludes if the interactant's attention is demanded elsewhere: the arrival at a destination, meeting consociates, or resuming former commitments suspended by spontaneous activities. Frustration and boredom also terminate involvement.

Lastly, some individuals engage in spontaneous momentry to see who is lured by sexual overtures rather than for erotic stimulation. Carefully generating enough interest to educe situational redefinitions, they withdraw as soon as someone responds to the bait. One individual related that he trolls for "fags" on Third Avenue during the workday lunch break. He walks up the street with a semi-erection. After given the eye, he saunters over to the nearest shop window and massages his penis through a pocket. After the "fag" moves next to him and reciprocates erotic signals, the "troller" moves on to the next conquest (from a conversation).

NOTES

1. Our use of "encounter" follows that of Goffman's (1961: 18) with one exception: there is no "openness to verbal communication" in the spontaneous setting.
2. Related to the observer by Dr. P. at his home in New Jersey.
3. John R is a personnel executive for a large retail food chain in the south. He was met through another contact in New York City.
4. At least 25 spontaneous street encounters have been witnessed by the observer either alone or in the company of homosexuals who were providing gay tours for his benefit.
5. Perhaps the best ethnography of hustling on the street is John Rechy's novel, *City of Night,* 1963.
6. For a chronicle of physical abuse of misplaced erotic endeavors, see "One Man's Story, Law Enforcement . . . or Sadism?" *The Advocate,* 1970.
7. Compare this strategem with a genuine "accidental" touch during a subway ride and the way utilized to disassociate any intentionality with it. See Hall, 1966.
8. Affectation of "civil inattention" has been extensively used as a technique of observation by this writer. For a discussion of this topic, see Goffman, B1963.
9. A black youth informed the observer that his sister frequently saw erotic encounters take place in subway cars as she commuted to and from work. He remembered one incident she related. One guy had shoved his hand into the other's trousers. She pretended not to notice, curious to see just how far they intended to go.

chapter 4

Erotic Oases

INTENTIONALITY
OF PARTICIPATION

The "surprise" and the feeling of "out-of-context" behavior of the spontaneous encounter arise from the unplanned, unexpected, and unanticipated nature of participation. The time and space zones within which they take place and the attire, grooming, appearance, and demeanor of the participant are entirely conventional.

Attendance at erotic oases represents a subtle shift from the randomness of spontaneous episodes. Although participation takes place within conventional rounds of activity and within ordinary settings, these territories are fixed into the social landscape and require adjustments in the individual's daily routine for attendance. Time must be

set aside for the travel to and from these destinations, as well as for the duration of attendance.

The most outstanding distinguishing characteristic of these territories is that they conduce to and are utilized for direct, physical sexual activity. For this reason, those present, particularly in the tearoom, are sexually suspect by the nonspontaneously involved. As areas of blatant sexuality, the erotic oasis is the first locational testament, albeit a muted one, in a series of more obvious placement statements (discussed below) to homosexual and erotic identities. Attendance ignites suspicion for those who wish to entertain it. And suspicion is the author for additional probing.

UMBRELLAS OF LEGITIMATION

Erotic oases share two important distinctive features that encourage open sexual activity. They are physically bounded, guarded, and contained by some sort of screening device that separates illicit behavior from conventional definitions and ·surroundings. Toilets, for example, have doors, often coin-locked. Trees and bushes cover erotic dialogues at beaches.[1] Inaccessible balconies, darkness, and the distraction of the movie envelope the theater scene.

Secondly, and most importantly, the taken-for-granted functions of these settings as perceived by the population at large serve as a cloak of concealment for illicit activity as long as nothing obtrudes within the scene to disturb the validity of these perceptions.[2] Setting functions extend a legitimating umbrella over any of the activity that transpires therein. The homosexual can therefore attend them for the functions they legitimately serve while, at the same time, transform them into theaters of erotic activities. In emergencies that threaten disclosure, the legitimating umbrella is unfolded to validate one's presence (e.g., "Gee officer, I was only taking a leak!"). Only in those cases where illicit behavior is so excessive that it cannot be rehidden under the cloak of everyday definitions are claims to setting legitimations unconvincing. Poorly executed covering tactics in public toilets, for example, result in arrest. In one observed toilet adventure, a policeman silently but suddenly pushed open a door to a Brooklyn subway john and found a young man standing in front of a commode (being fellated). As soon as he heard the door bang open, the young man whirled in a 45 degree angle away from the door, zipping up immediately. The cop yelled, "What the hell are you doing?" The youth, struggling for composure, stated he was merely adjusting his clothing. The cop stood cemented to the floor, the disbelief glaring from his face. However, he gave the young man, and his sexual counterpart in the commode stall two minutes to "get the fuck out — and don't ever let me see you here again!"

Setting legitimations are not merely reasserted but carried off with an air of complete casualness so that the taken-for-granted belief in normal functioning is portrayed with absolute conviction. At the slightest indication that an unidentified individual is entering the arena an air of normalcy, a quality of everything-as-usual, is instantly reimposed. The spontaneous involvement of the intruder is maximally encouraged until he drops cues that he is a fellow eroticist. In one observation, a group of approximately eight individuals had gathered around a "star" in various positions. Several participants were fellating each other while the star was practically stripped of his clothing, enjoying the sensation of a cascade of lips rummaging over his body. Faint footsteps shuffled outside the door. Penes were pulled out of mouths, pants hastily zipped; the "star" breathlessly pulled up, closed, and buttoned pants and shirt, while each participant broke from the clump of fleeting lovers to assume the "normal" air of conventional roles in the john. This occurred in a few seconds. When the door opened and the individual entered the situation appeared perfectly normal — individuals were found standing before urinals "apparently" urinating; blankly sitting on commodes; diligently washing hands; or "obviously" waiting with impatience for use of one or the other. All exhibited the air of the normal-meeting-mother-nature's-necessities-in-a-public-place. In this particular instance, the scene hastily reverted back into sexual frenzy after the newcomer's homosexuality was quickly discerned.

RIVAL POPULATIONS

Monetarily free or reasonably priced, various economic classes and ethnic groups increase the size and range of participants. Toilets, for example, cost no more than ten cents. Beaches are free or almost so, given parking costs or mass transit fees. The busiest movie houses are the $2.00 (or less) variety found in "decaying" neighborhoods. Given their functions, these settings attract a wide variety of social groups, the mix of which confounds the processes of community identification. Identities remain highly ambiguous until an elaborate, ritualistic set of cues and clues define them.[3]

Conventional dress is worn to erotic oases, further confounding the problem of distinguishing erotic others. On the other hand, everyday attire aids in legitimating one's presence during emergencies. In spite of suspiciously large numbers in tiny toilet cubicles, intruding police seem to ask few questions of those conventionally clothed who have successfully appropriated everyday behavior at the time of interruption.

Legitimate functioning versus unintended utilization of conventional settings used as erotic oases exacts great skill in alternating between involvement and noninvolvement, rapid recovery of conventional roles, and an acute sense of when to depart as the highly volatile situation fluctuates between suspicious-open-pretense-suspicious contexts, depending on who enters the setting. The entrance of ignorant conventionals quickly presses the players into roles that conform with conventional and expected performances. Any unfolding sexual drama is temporarily suspended until they depart. Their presence cannot last too long lest the carefully sustained charade be uncovered.

If the normal defecates or has problems urinating, detaining his departure, he will soon discover that the same individual has been wiping his hands for an inordinate length of time, or that the guy in front of the urinal has done nothing since the latter's arrival but hold his penis. If the normal detects the charade, it is always possible he will overreact and create problems. One individual, for instance, paced rapidly back and forth in a Brooklyn subway toilet, obviously distressed by an impending bowel movement. The john was crowded with eroticists impatiently awaiting his exit. Men occupied both commodes without audible evidence of "legitimately" using them. In spite of his sighs and fast pacing, no one moved. He finally left, muttering under his breath. Shortly thereafter, a transit police officer arrived and asked for identification.

If the normal (or presumed-to-be-straight individual) delays his departure too long, individuals begin leaving the scene — they run out of role material. Some may leave the setting, returning once the straight has left. Waiting for trains on the subway platform provides excellent cover for would-be participants postponing departure pending the clearance of a toilet. Others may depart for new areas of activity. Those remaining behind may hang on until the bitter end: either the normal exits or creates problems.

In any case, the active "maintenance" of conventional definitions of facility functioning does not necessarily interrupt all erotic communication. Eyes continue to communicate, often signaling the intention to stay on in spite of the obstruction, and may even reflect mounting interest and passion. The departure of the normal has not infrequently resulted in an explosion of wild sexuality due to pent-up tension.

A very visible sexual "competitiveness" exists between the desirable and undesirable players who haunt erotic oases that does not exist in the spontaneous situation, by definition, and which is obscured by norms of interaction in the types of settings discussed below. The presence of undesirable eroticists discourages others from engaging in sexual communications and transactions. A fat person, an effeminate type, or one of the corps of old men who always seem to be present may indefinitely suspend sexual interplay. Moods then fluctuate between frustration, boredom, anger, and sometimes outright hostility. One carefully neglected individual pounded his fists against a commode door in angry protestation over his exclusion from activities (whenever he approached anyone, they either moved to a new spot or left the toilet entirely).

THE TEAROOM: THE EROTIC OASIS
PAR EXCELLENCE

The public toilet is usually found wherever large numbers of people congregate for any length of time. The compact areas of utilization facilitate easy, intimate, very often visual appraisal of the partially exposed, uni-sex population. The reputations of some tearooms wildly fan erotic anticipations, predisposing those in attendance into precipitous and dramatic activities. However, not all tearooms host erotic activity. Certain physical and social arrangements preclude sexual behavior while others unwittingly encourage it.

Time and Timeliness

Many conveniences close for at least part of the 24-hour day. Institutional washrooms stay open as long as the organization functions. One toilet, for example, located in the basement concourse of a busy commercial building complex, conforms with general business hours of the companies located therein. Subway toilets are available for use between 7:00 a.m. and 9:00 p.m. A few are open 24 hours a day but, located at busy express stops and major points of transfer, they do not encourage "tearoom trade" (Humphreys, 1970).

Temporal peaks of activity in public toilets occur during breaktime, shifts in classes, and before and after class or work hours, acting as guides to the best time of attendance. Subway toilet activity peaks during rush hours. The tearoom in one IRT station is extremely busy between the hours of 7:00 and 9:30 a.m. and 4:00 to 7:00 p.m. The popular basement toilet in the Brooklyn Municipal Building busily pulsates the entire day. "Be here at 9:00 a.m. for blow job" is boldly scratched into the wall above the row of urinals.

Busy rush hours and class and lunch breaks mean more interruptions in tearoom activity than at other periods of the day. Watchfulness intensifies within these periods, increasing tension and circumspection during erotic maneuvering.

The passage of time inside a john without normal functioning is indirect evidence of erotic intentions. This time period seems to be related to the amount of time it takes an average individual to urinate. If he stands before the urinal slightly longer than the commonly understood "normal" time limit, suspicions mount —especially if the individual does not urinate at all.

Lastly, time contributes to the separation between the two moral possibly conflicting worlds of the erotic oasis — the conventional and the sexual. Moral distance between outside and inside identities is furnished by the brief interlude of conventionally established time for normal use of either urinal or commode. The entrant is able to reconnoiter the scene as he uses, or pretends to use, the facility. An aura of legitimacy covers this period if the entrant maintains the demeanor of the conventional-using-the-public-toilet-out-of-necessity, protecting him from illicit imputations unless the time spent exceeds commonly accepted limits.

Managing an Entrance

Only the "spontaneously" involved, or those in dire need, rush into the john. Arriving by train, the homosexual scans the station before getting off if heading for a subway toilet. A policeman on the platform means an inevitable interruption, and a particularly fateful one.[4] If a policeman is there, or if unattractive individuals hover near the door to the tearoom, the passenger journeys to the next tearoom. If the passenger must get off at a particular stop, he may sit down on a station bench, hoping for the departure of the unwanted company. When the area is vacated, he enters the toilet.

To impede observation of tearoom entrance by passengers on the train, the ever-wary public eroticist rides in the train car most distant from the tearoom door when the train is parked in the station. By the time he walks to the toilet door, the train will have pulled out of the station, wisking away any would-be witnesses. Another technique in obstructing uninvited observation is the "opposite walk" routine. The debarking individual walks in the opposite direction of the tearoom. Once the train is under way and pulling out of the station, a "feigned" surprise is exhibited for the potential unlooker with a "sudden" realization that one's direction is wrong. Again, the train has disappeared by the time one reaches the tearoom. The observer has followed individuals from one john to the next who employ these techniques at every stop. Having fixed their direction with an air of "distraction" (frequently toward a distant blank wall), they walk a few paces, abruptly look up (once the train is on the move), reverse direction, and head directly toward the tearoom. "Making calls" from telephone booths are also convenient and convincing "waiting" covers. No detail is too small to be omitted by the public eroticist when anticipating or engaging in public erotic encounters.

In contrast to the subway tearoom entrance, entry into the semi-public institutional tearooms lack much of the former's furtive quality. Only the presence of a uniformed guard creates circumspection. If security is present, entrance proceeds as usual (to reverse course after observation may create suspicion), but a timely departure within ordinary toilet use limits is demanded to avoid possible trouble.

Physical Features Conducive to Sexual Episodes

Toilets shielded by protective devices tend to be used for illicit sexual activity rather than those that have none. The longer the hall preceding the toilet, or the more numerous the obstacles to the main room of the convenience, the safer it becomes from surprise visitors. The most popular and active toilet in one Manhattan university, for example, is enclosed by a door and preceded by a fifteen-foot hallway that is also enclosed by a door. The layout grants lavish forewarning of new arrivals (the doors squeak when opened) and encourages extraordinary open sexuality. In addition to occasionally going naked, participants use "pot" and "poppers" (amylnitrite vapor) to accentuate sexual sensations.

Subway toilets are controlled by a coin-locked door.[5] The lock, and the noise coins make when deposited, serve as audible warning devices. The tingle near the door sends players into sudden flurries of activity to recover conventional roles.

In the underground toilet world, those who do not have the correct coin are not allowed in. Since the city is full of poverty wanderers seeking warm and dry places to sleep, public eroticists do not open doors for those who jingle them. Therefore, the possession of the correct change cannot be left to chance. The motivated homosexual makes sure that he has the correct change. Following an individual into a subway toilet at the Fulton Street complex, the observer looked over the depositor's shoulder and noted that he had at least $2.00 in nickels. Some individuals check their change before leaving one toilet setting for another, assuring entrance to the subsequent location.

If one does not have the correct coin, the individual waits for an arrival that does. As soon as the latter inserts the coin, the coinless individual follows him in at his expense.

That obstacles are crucial for the placement of erotic activities can be observed from the moral career of a toilet at a Queens stop on the IND line. Without a coin-locked door, it was free from public erotic activity. Even though the main room was preceded by a long hallway and separated from it by a door, ease of access discouraged public sex. The transit authority installed a coin-locked door at the entrance of the long hallway. The lock warns of impending interruptions and the long hallway supplies more than ample time for recovery tactics. Since installation, the toilet has become a highly popular setting for erotic activity. One very large public toilet that is free of charge is used for only voyeuristic purposes. The huge public restroom in Grand Central Station contains a long, trough-like urinal. Every lunch hour finds a line of voyeurs, shoulder-to-shoulder, massaging penes into erections, often masturbating to orgasm. No one, however, attempts to touch his neighbor. Voyeurism is a specific "sexual scene." Any attempt to touch a gazing neighbor defiles visual involvement and dissolves the carefully sustained tableau.

The Spartan furnishings of subway johns do not include mirrors. Interior decors of institutional johns do. Used for several functions, they aid in the reconnoiter of the setting. Grooming before a mirror increases the number of covering roles during moments of interruption. They are also used for indirect visual communication. With eyes signaling via reflection, unwanted surrounding others located on the sides miss the unfolding dialogue.

Institutional tearoom arrangements are kinder to privacy than those in the subway, furnishing dividers between urinals and commode stalls with doors enclosing each commode booth. Subway lavatories do not cater to these idiosyncracies, although doorless dividing walls separate commode booths. The lack of dividers and doors permit easy visual access to another's intentions and sexual interestingness. Ease in observation contributes to safety. For instance, a door encloses one of two commode booths in an IRT West Side subway tearoom. Cut off from all visual communication, those who sit there are invariably excluded from sexual activity. New arrivals to the scene note that the commode stall is occupied and, for the sake of safety, stride up to it, open the door, and affect "surprise" that it is occupied. After noting who is inside, they decide whether to remain in the john. If the commode stall is occupied by a "star," one or two others may try to join him in the booth. This is very dangerous. To make a timely withdrawal from a stall during a period of crisis, especially when partially undressed, creates too much noise as the commode door bangs in the confussion of exiting while simultaneously adjusting disheveled clothing.

Because institutional johns are not as heavily used as subway toilets, exotic sexual scenarios unfold that could not possibly be enacted in underground toilet situations. A small toilet tucked away on one of the upper floors of a Manhattan school, for instance, protected from surprise by a long preceding hallway followed by two consecutive doors placed close together, and only occasionally used during classes, is a favorite haunt of the community (for both students and all those who know of it). During one evening's observation, the individuals occupying two end commodes had completely stripped off their clothes. Stretched out under the partition dividing the commode stalls, they mutually fellated each other. Dangerously out of context, but extremely stimulating, the behavior encouraged five other attenders, all standing at urinals, to form their own group of mutual sodomy. An interruption occurred but all managed to recover conventional roles. As soon as the new entrant departed, the torrid scene resumed. The pair of nudes never attempted to recover any of their clothing during the interruption, not even shoes and socks. They simply sat on folded legs atop the toilet seat and centered their bodies in front of the closed door, to prevent being seen by any inquisitive intruder.

Another feature of the toilet is smell. The smell of urine is usually kept under control in institutional toilets. Not so in subway toilets where it can attain an intolerable foulness. The subway toilet at DeKalb Avenue, for instance, is so dirty that the stench of urine brings tears to the eyes. Still, public erotic work goes on. Odors do not seem to deter sexual activity. In fact, Dolly associates the smell of urine with the penis and oral sodomy. It is doubtful that the "suit set" on the East Side subway lines would use the DeKalb station toilet. However, they have been observed standing in a half-inch of water having sex in a flooded subway toilet. Furthermore, commodes sometimes become blocked, preventing flushing. The bowl sits for days filled with stinking excrement. This does not seem to deter public sex. Encounters go on as usual.

One last physical aspect of the toilet significantly contributes to erotic mobilization — graffiti. The existence of graffiti on toilet surfaces signifies to the novice and the experienced that the cubicle is an active setting. If no one is present upon arrival, the presence of graffiti suggests to the entrant that he delay departure, at least for awhile, and await developments. The observer found graffiti a reliable guide to active erotic settings because of this implicit meaning.

Aside from advertising times when notables will be present, or graphically illustrating unusual sexual practices (group sex or sadistic and/or masochistic practices), graffiti assists in the transformation of conventional attitudes into erotic ones. "Heady" sexual graphics predispose susceptible players into an excitable state. One subway toilet in Brooklyn, for example, is covered in graphic representations of figures engaging in oral and anal sodomy. Large penes, in both flaccid and erect states, crowd between the figures. "Puerto Rican with 10 inches, loves to get fucked"; "Horse cock, 11 x 2 inches, $10.00 blow job, $15.00 for fuck"; "black cock only, 8 inches and above"; etc., cram the remaining space. When a participant mounts one of the urinals, or sits in one of the stalls, his eyes cannot avoid these spirited epitaphs.

Graffiti can be mobile. Walking to the library one school evening, the observer ran into a fellow student who appeared in a great hurry. He puffed rigorously and seemed quite agitated. The observer asked him what was wrong. He replied that he was taking a "piss" break in the basement toilet of the library when he noticed a small piece of paper, folded in half for support, sitting on top of his urinal. Carefully printed on one side was "Turn around for blow job." He turned around and was amazed to see some guy's head peering out from under a commode booth located opposite the urinals. He flew into a rage and ran out to get the guard. By the time they returned, the public eroticist and the note had vanished.

Graffiti are instructive in the status and communications network of toilets. First, the penis and testes dominate most space. They are graphically represented wherever one looks. More importantly, if one compares the proportions of the penis and testes to the rest of the torso in these drawings, they assume enormous size. Largeness appears to be extremely important in the silent community.

Taking cues from the pictures on the walls and focusing on the interaction within the tearoom, the observer noted that those who brandished a large penis received the first and most attention. The size of the penis obviously affects the direction of erotic interest. Individual erotic styles sometimes deflect emphasis on the crude size of the penis if the situation lasts long enough. In a silent world, the size of the penis seems to have become the measuring rod of masculinity and virility and thus is a significant element in obtaining status (Parsons, 1951: 388). The larger the penis, the more virile the individual is thought to be, enhancing the amount of attention he receives. During a situation observed in a college john, a man in his 20s was fellating a student at the urinals. They were interrupted by a new entrant who assumed a position at a third urinal. The new arrival massaged his penis into an erection, and standing back, confidently displayed it. Impressed with the size, the previous fellator turned to it and commenced fellatio. His former partner quickly closed his trousers and departed, smarting under a severe loss of status.

Secondly, given the silent nature of tearoom and other public eroticism, the penis becomes an important factor in situational development. It can easily be seen and once erect denotes a firm interest in sexual activity.

Additionally, the penis plays a large part in the communications system. A person who has manipulated his penis into an erection and gazes at another actor or points the erection in the other individual's direction, covertly expresses a desire for and approbation of that person. The lack of such intimations declares a lack of interest or a wish to postpone activity until the toilet becomes less crowded (interest then devolves on eye communication). In communicating via the penis, the exhibitor offers the other person an opportunity to assess the tempter's virility and attractiveness. It also stimulates sexual proclivities.The succinct and ubiquitous "Show hard for blow job" found in almost every tearoom demonstrates the importance that the erect penis plays in the communications network, status system, and patterns of interaction in erotic oasis settings.

SEXUAL SCRIPTS INTRINSIC TO TOILET LAYOUTS

When a new arrival enters a tearoom, those already present silently question whether he is straight or homosexual. Once his homosexuality is determined, the next set of rapidly ensuing inquiries ponders the arrival's erotic identity. Because the silent void precludes verbal discourse, parts of the body and features of the setting environment are enlisted to help negotiate an answer to these puzzles.

Each facility of the restroom serves a specific function. Urinals accommodate urination, requiring a standing position for utilization. Although the commode can be used for both urination and bowel evacuation, it was intended for the latter. Usage prescribes pulling down the trousers and sitting on the bowl. Taking one or the other of the basic positions mean a great deal in establishing erotic identity. They are associated with sexual scripts.

The standing position at the urinal, for example, is associated with being serviced. The exposed penis can be quietly massaged while the individual devotes his attention to arranging a match through prudent visual communication. The subtle motion of the massaging arm can be seen by those present, signaling erotic intentions. When he finds a taker, he simply turns around to be serviced.

On the other hand, the commode dweller is seated. The face is crotch level. The position readily lends itself to the servicing role. From this advantageous, low-level position any excitation of the other participants can be seen as long as no obstacle compromises vision.

Very often, particularly in subway toilets, the physical plant of the setting enhances these positioning roles. Built perpendicular to the row of urinals, an individual occupying the commode located at the most acute position of the angle has full view of all those standing in front of the urinals. An interested urinal user signifies the desire to get "blown" merely by massaging the penis into an erection. Because the commode dweller is the only one who can see what is going on, except for the individual standing in front of the adjacent unit, he is able to quietly signify acquiescence simply by moving forward on the commode seat. In return, the urinal user turns around and gets fellated; that is, if all other attenders have been safely identified.

The toilet in the station of the first Brooklyn stop on the BMT line, for example, consisted of a long, narrow room (the toilet has been permanently closed for the past three years). The row of urinals and commodes joined in an acute right angle. The two innermost facilities were no more than one foot apart. If the commode dweller leaned forward when sitting, his head would touch the urinal. The toilet was extremely popular for this reason, with those two positions utilized most often. Communication between the two occupants tended to be blocked from the rest of the room. Exchanges resulted in direct sexual activity.

Servicee and servicor roles should not be oversimplified, nor should the implications resident in area functions be overblown. The "best" commode seat is frequently occupied by one of the host of undesirables who universally inhabit the public toilet world. Negotiating a viable sexual identity must somehow go forward without involving the ever-hungry individual. The individual posturing a sexual credibility will avoid the area in which the undesirable is located, depriving him of the functional messages he may have otherwise employed. Furthermore, many individuals do not avail themselves of either facility. Having quickly sized up the situation, they keep sexual options open by procuring a standing position along one of the walls, confusing initial cues. If sexual interest is aroused, communications are relayed through the eyes accompanied by subtle gesturing, e.g., hands quietly cupped over the crotch or inserted into the pockets followed by a slow, revolving movement suggesting quiescent masturbation.

Assuming positions at any of the functioning areas in the tearoom aid in the mutual definitions of those present. Subsequent information is necessary, however, for the congeries of gathered individuals to be drawn into an erotic transaction. The size of the penis, masculine bearing, youth, and physical build elevate or debilitate functional statements, necessitating adjustments in status claims. During an observation in Queens, a rather largely built, blond-haired man occupied a commode stall. Directly opposite and squarely in front of him stood a young man in his early 20s. Interested in the commode dweller, the youth openly massaged his penis through the trousers. The commode occupant responded by inserting a hand into his groin, signaling a reciprocal interest. He nodded to the stander to unzip and pull out his cock. When the latter did so, the sitting man stood up and displayed a much larger penis. It became apparent to the onlookers that the large man was not about to fellate the standing youth. The youth came to the same conclusion and commenced fellating the tall man.

THE META-COMMUNICATIONS
OF EROTIC POSTURING[6]

Silence, anonymity, and impersonality make strangers of tearoom participants except for those who attend regularly. With hundreds of public niches available for sexual encounters in New York City, the large public erotic population continually face the problem of identifying safe, interesting, and mutually responsive sexual partners. The processes of identification are complicated by the threat of imminent danger and the clandestine nature of signaling to interesting others while simultaneously holding at bay the host of undesirable others who are always ready to push through the perimeter of activity if they can.

As highly fluid settings, communications and the various stages of development attained by unfolding erotic dialogues are continuously interrupted, held in abeyance, frustrated, or reignited during the constant flow of arrivals and departures. Caught within this chaotic matrix are the sexual overtures that gradually stimulate open liaisons between some or many individuals who are engulfed in different depths of sexual engrossment. With each new arrival or departure, communications readjust to include or exclude the new arrival, and gloss over the void of the departed individual, particularly if he was desirable. The situation is an extraordinarily complex cauldron of activity.

If an undesirable individual stands before a urinal, the entrant may refuse to use the adjacent one. In order to signal his lack of interest and an intention of usurping the urinal area for his own use, the new arrival steps forward but immediately retreats to a wall position, cueing the undesired person that he had better urinate or vacate the facility. The individual is forced to leave the position rather quickly because the identity of the new arrival remains threateningly ambiguous. In one example a well-groomed individual in his mid-twenties and wearing an expensive grey suit casually walked into the subway john at 59th Street. Without looking at the three individuals present, he maintained an expressionless face and assumed a place along the wall. A urinal and a commode were available for use. Those present became exceedingly confused. The new entrant looked absolutely straight. The man at the urinal finally zipped up, washed his hands — taking many minutes — and finally exited with an exasperated look on his face. The man on the commode deeply concentrated in a type of self-involvement to prevent himself from staring at the new entrant. The third man fidgeted along an opposite wall, obviously becoming very nervous. Nonchalantly, the new entrant slipped both hands into his trouser pockets and began a massaging motion. The tension collapsed immediately. The two remaining eroticists vied with each other to secure the interest of the new arrival. Under such circumstances, anyone assuming a position along the wall while fixtures remain unoccupied is assumed to be "wise" or an inhibited straight that cannot function "normally" unless entirely alone.

If a toilet has three johns and an end one is occupied, the opposite unit is usually chosen. To select the one next to the occupied unit is to drop powerful cues that erotic adventures are desired. The privacy of meeting nature's necessities would suggest taking a position at the greatest distance unless the intentions of the individual are contrary to conventional use. Such a blatant move is considered a wide-open gesture and possibly an aggression, often prompting a retreat by the adjacent individual because the accepted and necessary fore-cueing has not taken place.

Propinquity, that is, the significant placement of oneself next to another attender, is another crucial signal in the intricate mesh of setting communications. Assuming a position next to a player without prior forewarning is almost an assault. Not to move away from the imposing placement, however, is indicative of acquiescence. Depending on the status of the entrant and the other identities in attendance, such moves may be gratifying and precipitate immediate sexual activity. Certainly an abrupt advance by a "star" is highly gratifying and always welcome. However, if an undesirable unceremoniously approaches, the overture threatens the recipient's status before the gathered ensemble unless the latter makes a visible rejection. To elicit undesirable attention creates serious doubt about the self's impressions. During an autumn afternoon observation in a Village john, six individuals had carefully jockeyed into a complementary network of positions. One slightly overweight man, however, moved about the already assimilated group, intently staring "down" the nearest individual. Sequentially, each individual studiously shunned his glances. As soon as he approached an individual, the player suspended erotic maneuvering and stood motionless. During this tug of war, an individual vacated a urinal position and placed himself next to a man on the opposite wall. No visual communication preceded the unexpected move. None seemed to pass as they stood motionlessly side by side. Carefully ignoring each other (and warily watching the freefloating interloper), their hands touched. Without further ado, they turned backs to the assemblage (a strong indication that they did not wish to be joined by anyone else) and carried out a heavy sexual scene. The only communication between them was the urinal dweller's thoughtful placement and the meaning inferred from it.

The most insignificant cue dramatically contributes to the building and definition of a new arrival's imputed identity. In a cubicle already "positioned" by several eroticists, the atmosphere hangs heavy with anticipation as they wait — hope — for some sign that the new arrival is a fellow homosexual. For example, "Big Bob" occupied a commode stall in a BMT subway toilet in Brooklyn. Trousers carelessly hung about his calves as he sat reading a newspaper. His legs hung open, permitting visual perception of a large penis. He had been alone in the tearoom for about a half hour when a coin dropped into the lock. In struggled a youthful man carrying an obviously heavy parcel. The young man passed Bob's booth to the only other commode, which was unoccupied. When doing so, he quickly glanced at Bob. Bob thought he was gay but did not move, waiting for firmer signs. The glance could have been merely reactive. The man deposited the parcel on the floor and sat down. After squatting for sometime on the commode, he peered through the peep hole drilled into the dividing partition. Bob noted the shadow over the hole but continued reading. No further cue was necessary — the guy was a homosexual and wanted activity. However, the entrant did not know who Bob was. The hole was shadowed frequently thereafter in his attempt to elicit a response from Bob. Between gazes through the hole, the youth would lean way back on his seat, hoping Bob would look through the hole while he exhibited his penis. Bob did not move. In apparent exasperation, the youth made sounds of completing nature's necessities. After audibly wiping his anus with toilet tissue, he flushed the toilet repeatedly, and pulled up his trousers. Bob remained impassive. The youth then passed Bob's commode to wash his hands at the sink located on the opposite wall (a familiar strategy utilized by eroticists when they want to look at the person in the next booth). As he passed, he glanced again at Bob. Bob remained motionless, absorbed in the newspaper. When passing back to his commode stall, he looked once more. Bob ignored him. The youth created a great fanfare while putting on his jacket, assuring Bob he was preparing to leave. He was now sending cues at a furious rate. Bob's carefully studied negligence, and failure to use the commode "normally" obviously raised suspicion in the young man's mind. By this time, the youth had noted Bob's penis and tried his best to place Bob. Finally, he stood in front of the commodes, slightly to the right of Bob's door. Both could see each other. At first Bob continued the charade of reading the paper. The youth fidgeted, looking now at Bob and then away before Bob caught him looking. He gave every appearance of being excessively nervous. Finally, Bob allowed one hand to touch the tip of his penis while distractedly gazing at the newspaper (he was not reading). The youth seized on this single cue. Within an instant and without further cueing, he grabbed Bob's penis and fellated it. Bob and the youth became friends after the incident. When the youth recounts the meeting, he vividly recalls how nervous it made him. He felt sure that Bob was straight or a vice cop, baiting him to play out his hand and then "pow."[7] However, once he saw Bob's large penis, he decided to go the limit.

If the new arrival selects to occupy a commode stall, several techniques prevail by which he signifies erotic intentions. He may casually drop his trousers to below the knees, momentarily exposing the genitals to the present ensemble. Few individuals use this conspicuous exposure except those who want to show off a large penis. The individual, for example, who regularly appears in Queens' IND subway toilets, sits on the commode with trousers draped about his ankles, back arched so that the shoulders brace against the wall and the torso bends in such a way that his rather long penis visibly shouts for attention. This is an open invitation for anyone to "chance" an approach and fellate him. The "openness" of the posture informs all that he expects to get "sucked off only." His particular "sexual scene" is having as many individuals as possible fellate him just short of orgasm. In anyone setting among the same audience, increasing numbers of fellators mean an expanded sense of prestige and status.

The usual commode dweller sits down on the seat without exposing himself. Trousers hug the thighs. In doing so, he sustains conventional demeanor, giving himself time to survey the range of those present before dropping cues to who he is.

Selection of a commode depends on its location with reference to the ready accessibility of others present. The individual avoids any cubicle with a door because it suspends visual communication with others. Commode dwellers are easily excluded from developing dialogues between urinal and wall participants. With restricted vision, they see only what is in front of them. Immobility prevents expeditious relocation.

If a "scene" moves out of his sightlines, an exasperated commode occupant stands up (trousers still draped around the ankles), massages his joint, and looks around the corner of the stall at the transpiring action. This recourse is considered offensive, breaking the tacitly accepted rule of sexual acquiescence through quiet cueing. The fact that the "scene" takes place out of visual range strongly suggests that the participants have purposely excluded him. His uninvited assay is unmistakably disruptive as the actors grimace and hurl heavy sighs of disgust at him, causing him embarrassment and earning him their unremitting disdain. One elderly man in a Manhattan IRT toilet actually chased an encountering threesome about the room. As he advanced, they moved. He tried again, they relocated again. The third interruption was the last straw — all three interactants left in a huff (two journeyed to a tearoom two stops away).[8]

In large tearooms located in institutions, the commode is

the preferred choice of location. The bright lights that highlight physical defects, the presence of mirrors on the wall that permit immediate, comprehensive views of the entire john (except for the enclosed commode stall), and inadequate warning of new arrivals (no coin lock on the door), encourage commode use. The door of the commode stall becomes a major protective device.

Initial selection depends on the availability of free ones. If only one commode is occupied, the next one to it is the logical choice. To choose it makes an implicit statement of erotic intentions.

Dividers between commodes are not built to the floor. A space of 18 inches separate the divider from the floor. This space is vital for communication and sexual activity.

The homosexual determines which commode is occupied by stooping down to floor level and noting where shoes are placed. This is done only if the outside area of the toilet is empty. Some arrivals try each commode door, not only to test it for vacancy (occupied booths are locked from the inside), but to see who is on the other side by peering through various cracks around the door. If the person inside seems interesting and the booth next to him is vacant, he takes it.

Having selected a commode stall and signaling initial statements predicated by the selection, a period of time elapses before more direct overtures unfold. This time period is one of silence, broken at most by urination. "Normal" functioning would spoil erotic prospects. When both individuals ascertain that their neighbor is not functioning "normally," feet begin to signal. The slightest shuffle of a shoe, a move usually toward the occupied commode, initiates communication. After mutual communications are reciprocated, hands slip under the divider for a tactile investigation of the legs, thighs, and genitals. This is usually a mutual exchange. The characteristics of these human parts form identity images based in large part from previous episodes. The full identity of the individual can be ascertained if the individual gets on his hands and knees and swings his head underneath the divider. If this is not done, tactile investigations may contain surprises when the individual is finally seen (if he is seen at all). During one episode, a youth looked under the divider and thought he saw firm legs on a rather youthful body (he did not look up at the face). Grabbing the man's calf hard, the informant signaled the next occupant to slip his torso under the divider so he could fellate him. The guy complied, and Mr. X enjoyed the encounter. However, as the man prepared to leave the toilet, he knocked on X's door to thank him. When X opened the door, he was overcome with despair. Before him stood an old man in his late 60s, white, wrinkled, and haggard. As he smiled his thanks, a set of stained, chipped and decaying teeth spread between the parting lips. Mr. X vowed never to fellate anyone again without seeing him in person and in good light.

If foot signals continue past a certain time period and no hand movement follows, the occupant might write a note. This has only been observed in institutional johns. A sample of recovered notes read: "What do you like to do?"; "Do you suck?"; "Take your shirt off."; "Stick your dick under and I'll suck it"; "Do you suck or fuck? I like to eat ass, are you interested?"; "Put your ass near the wall and I'll fuck it"; "Let's go to the 6th floor john where it's not so busy."

Once hands have passed under the dividing walls and have investigated the interesting segments of the human anatomy, one or both participants signal the other to slide the torso underneath the partition for fellatio. To avoid difficult body postures, the doors to the stalls are occasionally held ajar, and sex takes place in front of the stalls. To do so requires extraordinary attention to the possibility of interruption, given the length of time restricted ambulation takes to safely get back inside, robbing the episode of sexual abandon.

A SUBWAY ENCOUNTER

No amount of written description can capture the subtle, complex contrapuntal web of communications that take place during tearoom eroticism. A few negotiations are apparent, but most are conducted under a veil of indifference. Careful placement, flow of time, casual eye contact (rapidly fluctuating between penetrating and indifferent stares), gestural language — subtle to gross — touch, and finally sexual engrossment orchestrate the fugue-like stages of the sexual scenario. Orgasm or intrusion concludes it. Silence, of course, thunders supreme. During erotic maneuvering, any observer would note, as the participants routinely do, who is included in and diligently excluded from various dialogues. Some individuals receive more overtures than others. In fact, someone may receive all the attention. Nonpersons are considered not present. Vicarious participation is usually tolerated, and makes a positive erotic contribution if vigorous masturbation mirrors the waves of sexual activity. The ostracized are permitted to look, in some cases, but never allowed to touch. The individual who prefers only to watch remains on the periphery of the scene of action.

The scripts of the players can be anticipated from initial placement in the toilet, but actual enactment contains surprises. Only after the continuum of desirability has been negotiated do the roles of the actors become firm.

The following encounter took place in a subway toilet located in a local stop south of one of the most active subway toilets in the city. The observation was made during the summer months of 1969. As a local stop, the station is relatively quiet most of the day except for rush hours. The time of observation was approximately 4:00 p.m., the beginning of the evening rush hour.

The toilet is small. The coin-locked door opens into a narrowly square (4 x 4 foot) vestibule. The entrance between vestibule and toilet is doorless. The main room of the toilet measures approximately eight feet by twelve feet. To the left of the entrance, one foot from the doorless frame, is a sink. Two urinals are located three feet from the sink on the same wall. Four feet from the urinals, on the wall facing the urinals and directly facing the entrance, sit two commode stalls. A door encloses the stall closest to the urinals. A large "glory hole" and several peep holes have been gouged through it.[10] The adjacent commode stall is door-less. Both commodes provide visual access to the entire room, one by virtue of the glory hole, the other because it is doorless. Little graffiti decorate the main chamber. Large drawings of genitals and erotic positions smother the walls in the enclosed commode stall.

When the observer arrived at the toilet, a red-headed man, about 25 years old, dressed in a short-sleeved shirt and jeans, occupied the urinal located nearest the enclosed commode stall. Looking underneath the door of the commode as he walked toward it, the observer noted that it was occupied. Feigning ignorance, the observer opened the door, discovered a small, black man of about 50 years of age inside, mumbled an apology for the intrusion, and decided to occupy the free commode. The observer wore his usual tearoom observation attire: tight-fitting teeshirt, baggy, unkempt trousers, and Army-issue black shoes. He had found that this combination of attire attracted little interest during erotic observations but did not prove offensive enough to inhibit others from erotic maneuvering.

After sitting on the commode seat, the observer pulled his trousers up to the thighs. While he busied himself, "Reds" flushed and reflushed the urinal, legitimating his continuing presence there. He also began evaluating the observer. Because the observer did nothing but sit, making no sound of "normal" performance, and because no one else was present except for the old man whom Reds entirely ignored, Reds occasionally glanced toward the observer. Simultaneously, he pulled slightly away from the urinal displaying the shaft of an erect penis. The observer studiously avoided looking his way.[11]

Trying another strategy, Reds zipped up and moved to the opposite wall from the urinals, standing only a few feet from the observer. Standing motionless a few moments, and repeatedly glancing at the observer, he slowly lifted his hand toward the observer. The observer quietly shook his head "no," making sure not to look at Reds. The rejection seemed to have no effect; the hand remained extended. Luckily, however, before the observer found it necessary to vacate the room, a coin was deposited in the lock. Reds flew back to the urinal, unzipped, and flushed the urinal. While doing so, a large man, at least six feet tall, walked in and assumed a position in front of the urinal next to Reds.

The new arrival was obviously a weight-lifter. Large muscles bulged beneath a tight form-fitting blue shirt. His jeans seemed almost unable to contain the well-developed leg muscles. He had short-cropped black hair and blue eyes. A leather band choked the left wrist.

"Muscles" maintained conventional demeanor until he could ascertain who was present. The occupant of the door-enclosed commode stall obviously bothered him. He quietly looked at it several times. He urinated, but continued standing in front of the urinal after finishing. Seconds passed. He did not massage his penis. Looking at the blank wall in front of him, he probably used side vision to see if any movement was taking place. During this time, Reds glanced at him without turning his head. As seconds dragged into minutes, Reds became bolder. He started to massage his penis. The activity could be noted by the observer by watching the rear of Reds' active arm. Cautiously, inch by inch, Reds' head turned toward Muscles. Muscles made no reciprocating movement, but side vision no doubt informed him of what was happening. Reds dropped his left hand and arm to his side, a preparatory gesture signalling the desire to grab a neighbor's penis. Muscles responded by turning toward Reds with visual glances that encompassed the whole room. Nodding to Reds, he inquired who was behind the door-enclosed booth. Reds shrugged, indicating the occupant was "okay." Next, Muscle looked at the observer. The observer looked his way with what he thought was a noncommital glance. To his amazement, Muscles continued looking at him, massaging his penis into an erection. Once erect, he slowly pulled away from the urinal, exhibiting a penis that was longer and thicker than Reds.

At this time, Reds' interest in Muscle intensified. Vigorously massaging his cock, he pulled at least a foot away from the urinal and turned full-face to Muscles. The latter however was posturing toward the observer. The observer decided to look interested in Reds to discourage any direct advance from Muscles. For about three minutes, the situation froze into this triangle of interest (the individual in the door-enclosed booth was taking in the urinal scene and masturbating rapidly).

The roar of an arriving train broke the tension and absorption of the triangular relationship before it degenerated into frustration or boredom. Muscles and Reds turned toward respective urinals, ceasing communication. Eyes blankly focused on the wall as each listened for the sound of new arrivals. The observer continued sitting as before.

The doors of the subway train were heard closing. The sound of acceleration screamed upward when a coin dropped into the lock. Two men entered, one black, the other white. The black male was tall, lean, and very dark. The white male, also tall, was somewhat heavier in build. He had sandy colored hair, pale skin, brown eyes, and wore glasses. The black wore a long-sleeved red shirt and navy blue trousers. The white guy was wearing a short sleeve, western print shirt, and tight bluejeans that prominently outlined a large groin bulge. Dark brown boots hugged his feet.

Upon the new entrants' arrival, Muscles and Reds flushed respective urinals several times. The new arrivals assumed positions along the wall opposite the urinals several feet from each other (indicating little initial interest in each other), and "apparently" waited for one of the facilities to become free. During these movements, each quickly scanned the commode area. The problem of the unidentified individual behind the door-closed booth drew continued attention. Unable to endure the suspense, the white man casually walked over to it, opened the door wide, noted the occupant, excused himself, and returned to his original position. This maneuver confirmed the investigator's erotic intentions to the others present although his carefully arranged penis raised suspicions as soon as he entered. The black male continued to wait along the wall for one of the facilities, impatiently shifting body weight from leg to leg.

Reds and Muscles simultaneously decided to vacate

positions. First Reds and then Muscles flushed the urinal for the last time, and took a position along the wall. Reds stood close to where the observer sat. Muscles assumed a position two feet from Reds. The black male moved to one of the urinals (without urinating). "Glasses" left his original position and leaned against the sink. By doing so, he had full view of black's penis and the rest of the ensemble.

A surprise coin was heard to drop into the lock (no train had pulled into the station). Reds quickly opened his trousers and pretended to be tucking in his shirt. Muscles turned toward the door, assuming the role of a person about to depart from the toilet. Glasses turned to the sink and washed his hands. Mr. Black remained motionless in front of the urinal. Mr. X in the door-enclosed booth pulled back on his seat. The observer began feeling panicky — too many men in the small toilet. Any entering cop would immediately size up the situation.

A short male, dressed in loose fitting jeans, and a nondescript, slightly soiled, short-sleeve white shirt, opened the door. When he entered he could not help but note the number of people in the john. Instead of entering the main room, he hovered in the vestibule to make possible a hasty departure should the law arrive. The choice of location tipped everyone off that he was probably a homosexual. He stood in front of the door, now and again peering out through the slanted slats.

Covering roles carried out when the new entrant arrived were promptly discarded. However, no movement toward eroticism could be discerned. Black continued to occupy a position in front of the urinal, Glasses again leaned against the sink (nicely propping up and highlighting his basket), and Reds and Muscles moved back into their wall positions. An air of indifference radiated from all except for Reds, who maintained his interest in Muscles, although his eyes repeatedly looked at Glasses' bulging groin.

Time slowly passed in this frozen setting. Although looks and glances darted between the participants, they did not solidify into a visual dialogue. Another train arrived in the station. When it pulled out, a coin dropped into the lock and everyone repeated their role in the conventional charade. Two males entered the john. One was dressed in jeans and a tight-fitting red jersey. He too lifted weights, but was less developed than Muscles.

The other individual wore a suit. Blue blazer, white shirt, gray trousers and a bright tie became the tall individual who was a slim, six foot two or three inches tall. Brown, wavy hair crested a well-tanned face. Blazing brown eyes flashed from one individual to the next as he walked into the main chamber. He stood in front of the free urinal. The other arrival took a position on the already-crowded wall.

Mr. Black departed, apparently tired of waiting for an overture, and becoming tense by the growing numbers of people. Once the outside door had closed (the individual standing in the vestibule gave the door an extra shove to make sure it was locked) Reds reclaimed the free urinal after the other new arrival failed to do so.

He began introductory cueing by looking at Suit. He massaged his penis. Suit looked at him, at the penis, and then around the room. His attention riveted on Muscles. Muscles continued an air of indifference. Glasses looked with interest at the other entrant, who meanwhile glanced at the guy in the vestibule. Mr. X in the door-enclosed commode stall had resumed the forward position, and was again masturbating.

Without forewarning, Suit closed his trousers, walked over to Muscles, opened Muscles' trousers, pulled out his penis, and fellated him. Reds hurried over to the action, penis in hand, but was not invited to join. Excluded, he anxiously stood there and watched. Muscles, by the way, made no movement whatsoever. Because no gestural cueing preceded Suit's advance, he was unprepared for the sudden assault. No rejection followed and certainly no displeasure because an erection quickly developed. He obviously enjoyed the advance. Suit fellated Muscles into orgasm.

Emotional contagion prompted further interaction among the rest of the ensemble. Glasses rubbed his penis into an erection. Without exposing it, he walked over to the individual still standing along the wall, and began fondling him. The new entrant alternated between touching Glasses' penis, and exhibiting visual interest in the man in the vestibule. The latter returned a similar interest and joined the twosome. No sooner were they together — Glasses touching the new entrant's crotch, and the new entrant and the vestibule occupant exchanging looks and touches — when Muscles groaned in orgasm. Suit continued fellating until the penis went flaccid. He then returned to the urinal, spat out the sperm, wiped his mouth with a handkerchief, and headed for the door. The threesome quickly split up, moving out of the door's visual range. Suit departed. Shortly thereafter, Muscles followed.[12] Before Suit opened the door Reds rushed over to a urinal. He remained there as the threesome reunited after the door closed (which was again shoved to make sure that it was locked). He furtively watched the unfolding scene, casually masturbating.

When Glasses again walked over to the object of interest, he had his penis in hand. It was large. The new entrant displayed more interest than previously. He fondled it but continued touching the vestibule occupant (who never returned the touch, but never moved away). Without warning, Glasses pulled out the new entrant's cock, and started to fellate him. The new entrant became very excited, rapidly touching the vestibule occupant. After a few moments of fellatio, he motioned Glasses to stand up. When he did, the new entrant went down on Glasses, and fellated vigorously. Glasses began to tremble, grabbing at and pulling on the body of the fellator. Apparently near climax, he stopped the new entrant from further fellatio. No sooner was the latter's head up when Glasses resumed fellating him. This time, Glasses would not stop sucking when prodded to. Seconds thereafter, the new entrant grabbed the head of Glasses and shoved it down hard on his penis. He did this repeatedly during ejaculation. Glasses became very agitated with each new thrust, masturbating himself very rapidly. The vestibule occupant just stared, having been left out of the rapidly unfolding drama. After orgasm, the two simply hung over each other for a few seconds. Withdrawing gradually, they continued touching each other and smiled. The new entrant walked over to the observer's booth, excused himself as he reached for toilet tissue, walked back to his original position, wiped off in front of Glasses, threw the tissue on the floor, adjusted trousers, caressed Glasses, kissing him lightly on the lips, and departed. The arrival of a train sounded shortly thereafter and he probably boarded it.

The vestibule occupant went back to the position behind the door. Glasses adjusted his clothing, and leaned against the sink. Reds intently looked at him obviously hoping for some action at last. However, Glasses ignored him. Another rejection! The lack of interest between those present became oppressive. Not a glance passed between them. When another train pulled into the station, the vestibule occupant and Glasses withdrew.

By this time, the observer was weary. He had been sitting for over an hour. He determined to withdraw as soon as the next train arrived. As he got up, Reds turned and looked hopeful. The observer hurried dressing and rushed out of the cubicle.

SIGNALS OF PERIL

When engaging in public eroticism, the background sounds of the everyday world that are usually assimilated in the unattended matters of one's daily rounds of activity are transformed by the homosexual into vividly audible warnings of impending interruption and possible danger. The arrival of a train in the subway station signals caution. Train arrivals signify inevitable interruptions. Participants stop serious erotic activity until sufficient time has elapsed that would permit the entrance of any new arrivals. There is a commonsense definition of how much time is required for such entrances and community members "intuitively" know its parameters. For example, a toilet on the IRT subway line was crammed with ten people. Two men took turns in mutual (oral) sodomy. One of the pair held a third party's penis in his hand. The remaining seven engaged in various petting activities. A train roared into the station. One of the fellating individuals lifted his head from the other's penis, motioning the other members to be careful. Activity froze. Hands continued to grasp and even slightly massage penes but fellatio ceased. Erections remained firm, but active eroticism continued suspended. When the train pulled out of the station, and all footsteps on the subway platform faded toward the station exit, and sufficient time passed without interruption, the pregnant tableau burst back into life.

The sound of opening and closing doors in institutional hallways performs the same signaling service. Someone may be approaching the tearoom.

One sound that not only suspends activity but readily dissolves situational involvement is the noise of a transit policeman's radio. As soon as it is heard individuals begin withdrawing from the scene, anticipating the unavoidable, disruptive visitor.

THE MORALS AND MANNERS IN FACELESS ENGAGEMENTS: "THE GLORY HOLE"

The glory hole is an example of social interaction in total anonymity on the one hand, and extreme ideal typifications of erotic identities on the other. Interaction depends on two or at most three parts of the body: the penis and the mouth or anus. A wall separates interactants, completely isolating them from each other except for contact between penis and mouth or anus.

Not a peep hole, the glory hole must be large enough to permit the easy passage of the penis yet small enough to restrict visual means of identifying the individual on the other side. Although the mid-range of the torso can be seen through the glory hole, particularly the genital area, and some characteristics of the body — color of skin, weight, amount of hair on the body, and age — facial identification is usually impossible. Members of the episode remain faceless.

The glory hole is found in public toilets and is subject to the complex host of factors that affect convenience activity. The aperture of the glory hole and the small, constrained visual range of the other side of the hole become the focal point of all sociation. Because of restricted vision, the genitals on the opposite side of the apperture could belong to the self's most fantastic sexual ideal. The size of the penis and testes, their shape and color, and the hand that manipulates them, as well as the torso's color, size, and shape, and the minimum of mannerisms that can be ascertained through the hole, either aid or destroy the identity illusions that the self entertains of other.

The key element in glory hole activity is total, anonymous sexual activity. Communications between participants flow only through the aperture. Initial cues to erotic interest are few. If the occupant of a booth does not cover up the hole with toilet tissue, it is assumed that an implicit interest in a sexual dialogue exists. Straight males do not use a commode with a glory hole bored through its wall if others are free that do not have one. If a straight individual must utilize such a booth, he leans forward to block the visual accessibility of the glory hole. In so doing, he also covers the genital area of his body by virtue of the angle he assumes.

According to H.G., blatant communications rarely take place initially. The arm nearest the aperture is usually placed in such a way that it partially blocks the view of any activity. In this way, an active arm can be partially seen moving, appearing as if the guy is masturbating, when in fact he is simulating the activity for signaling purposes. When reciprocal activity takes place by the next occupant, the arm is removed and an erect penis displayed.

The only crucial status occupied by the actors is related to the size and shape of the penis. If either is not satisfied with the other's penis, he discontinues signaling and waits for the other occupant to leave. He may tire of waiting and vacate the stall for more promising territory. Once sexual activity commences, it tends to be rather standard. The penis slips through the hole. Fellatio follows, usually to orgasm.

Glory hole interaction is often one-sided (servicor or servicee), but it can be mutual. In the case of mutual activity, the servicor gives off cues to his hypothetical identity when slipping his penis through the hole, destroying part of the mystery behind the "mouth." During these faceless engagements, a wart, sore, or blemish on the penis, a peculiar twist in its shaft, or the fact that it is black instead of white, or vice versa, will destroy the "identity" of the inserting party where, if he had not inserted his penis and remained a servicor, the mystery would have remained intact. Of course, exposing his penis could enhance identity simply by surpassing the expectations of the other interactant.

Recovery of conventional identity is relatively easy in the glory hole context. Given the fact that the commode stalls have doors, penes can be withdrawn readily and invisibly upon intrusion. In fact, given the privacy of the context, erotic dialogues sometime continue while unsuspecting intruders take care of business on the outside. One youthful student related to the observer that he takes particular joy in continuing fellatio when danger is at hand. When he fellates someone through a glory hole, he seizes the calves of the servicee underneath the dividing wall (where possible) and holds him firm when intrusion occurs. Most times, only brief resistance is encountered. The real danger during these moments are the "moaners." "Some guys moan and groan when they shoot. Probably something they're not aware of. If he does and someone's in the john, you better hustle your ass out of there as soon as the guy outside leaves (and brings back the police or security)." (From an informal interview with an anonymous artist of the glory-hole scene.)

Sexual activity usually stops upon intrusion. During sexual encounters, the feet are pointed in the wrong direction. Commode dividers and walls, rarely built to the floor, permit visual access to the feet of the occupants. Gay others and security agents always stoop down and look underneath the dividers when they first enter the john to check if anything is going on. The direction of the feet can be hidden by carefully placing an attache case, shopping bag, or pile of books in a position that blocks perception of them. If cracks separate the door from its frame, visible access demand respect for conventional codes of behavior. Hanging coats and other articles of clothing behind cracks prevent visibility. If a servicor is noisy in fellating, all preventions fail.

In summation, the glory hole setting is one of intensive sexual stimulation. As mentioned above, social identities remain anonymous and faceless. Only large categorical characteristics are apparent. The limited area of communication and interaction circumscribe visual focus, narrowly circumscribing attention. The topic of interaction is accordingly intensified and the sexual scenes that ensue are extremely sensual and brief in nature. Some other settings offer similar total anonymity because of lack of light — the trucks, "back rooms" in pig parlors,[13] and the orgy room in the baths — but according to informants no setting attains the same magnitude of sensuosity.

NOTES

1. Although daytime cruising takes place in parks (e.g., Central Park), the widespread use of parks occurs at night. Daytime cruising is influenced by conventional concerns and affects cruising behavior. It is covered in the present discussion with one important omission: the manipulation of attire for cueing purposes. This topic, and that of nighttime cruising in parks will be discussed under "nocturnal visits." Because attendance at movies usually takes place during leisure time, they too will be subsumed in the same subsequent chapter. Beaches where direct sexual concourse occurs are extremely isolated. For all intents and purposes, they are "sheltered settings" and will be discussed in the chapter devoted to that topic.
2. See Cohen (1966: 109–110) for a discussion on concomitant legitimate and illegitimate opportunities within a given context.
3. For similar studies of populations who use covert signaling, see Winick and Kinsie, 1971, and Milner, 1972.
4. The incongruity between the sudden "rush" of police and the taut, absolutely convincing conventionality portrayed by eroticists who don't flinch from the surprise visitors, nicely outlines the game each is

playing. A straight in similar circumstances could not help but overreact. Discovering the toilet overcrowded but nothing going on, the police simply ask all those present to vacate the premises — a pallid conclusion to a dramatic entrance.

5. In the spring of 1977, coin-locks were removed from all public toilets, including subway johns, in conformance with a new statute passed by the New York State legislature.

6. Professor John Johnson must be credited with the succinct labeling of erotic posturing as "meta-communications."

7. Police in New York City no longer employ entrapment as a technique in arresting homosexuals. They do in Los Angeles. See "Hollywood vice: Cops or robbers? two ask," *The Advocate*, 1972: 8.

8. A favorite technique in "escaping" undesirables, either the police or unwanted would-be participants, is to move two or three stops away from the previous station rather than only one. The unwanted individual usually travels only one stop further to nourish an injured pride. The police make every stop.

9. The observer overheard an eroticist reassure a tense participant in this tearoom by stating, "Don't worry, they never bother you here."

10. A "glory hole" is an aperture bored through a dividing wall or door that is large enough and placed at the correct "average" height to permit the easy passage of the penis and perhaps (rarely) the testicles. They are found only in toilets.

11. The observer was unable to understand why others found him attractive during this observation. During other observations while wearing the same drag, he was ignored. The only difference about his appearance was a summer tan. The observation gear usually dissuaded any interest among the erotic participants.

12. Rarely do participants leave together or in groups. To do so is thought to draw unwanted attention. Only the arrival of the police prompts departures "en masse."

13. Dr. E labeled these settings "pig parlors" (described below) when he reported their existence to the observer. Others called them after-hour bars, bars with "suck" rooms, orgy room bars, and various other names. The outstanding and singular difference from the gay bar is the back room explicitly furnished by management for sexual encounters. Dr. E called them pig parlors because the management failed to provide adequate facilities to clean up after sexual encounters, and because of the various, often loud, concert of sucking sounds that emanate from the room, reminding him (a former farmer) of pigs at feed.

chapter 5

Nocturnal Visits to Peripheral Times and Spaces

TEMPORAL AND SPATIAL CLUES TO SEXUAL IDENTITIES

Previously discussed settings that host homosexual erotic activity are squeezed into the routines of the conventional world within commonly accepted standards of attire, imagery, and self-presentations. Sexual conquests are woven in and around everyday contexts where conventional fabric is carefully rethreaded into erotic designs. Within this framework of utilization the commonsense, taken-for-granted everyday world consists of both the mundanely commonplace and the estatically erotic. However, the union is not a stable one. Although conventional imagery acts as a protective shield for erotic activity it tends to confound erotic identification.

To avoid misdirecting erotic efforts, elaborate communications precede even the slightest indication of secret intentions. Spontaneous encounters congeal only randomly and then frustrate suddenly inflamed passions because of contextual restraints. Identities remain highly ambiguous and always constrained, given the thorough conventionality of the setting. Erotic oases furnish enough obstacles to encourage highly dramatic episodes and even veil them with a legitimating cover. However, the flux between homosexual and heterosexual audiences, and the ever-present threat of interruption, contradictorily heightens ardor that is nullified by momentary interference.

Approaching leisure time erotic activity by the silent community, time and space are utilized to separate the conventional world from the erotic one.[1] Identities become more openly identifiable, less conjectural, if placed within certain temporal and spatial contexts (for a discussion of identifying strangers through locational cues, see Lofland, 1973). Mere attendance at night spots, for example, generates rather open homosexual statements because of the unusual time of attendance at areas not normally visited at such times by "normal" society.

Nocturnal visits to peripheral settings of the urban landscape are made by the homosexual, by definition, under the mantle of darkness. The late hour of attendance significantly contributes to the peripheral quality of the setting. Fear of being mugged, for instance, drives most normals from parks before darkness descends. The aforementioned trucks swing into full gear around 2:00 a.m. They swell with activity after the bars close at 4:00 a.m. A Brooklyn park studied for many months remains empty until about 10:00 p.m. The hours of 11:30 p.m. to 3:00 a.m. are its busiest.

A second characteristic of peripheral settings is geographic isolation, a solitude reinforced by the late hour of visitation. The trucks are parked in a warehouse section of the West Village. Surrounding streets are deserted after dusk with the exception of gay bar traffic traveling to nearby bars. The decaying pier hugs a small portion of city real estate along the Hudson River under the closed and unused West Side Highway. Traffic, both vehicular and pedestrian, withers with the advance of the clock.

Late hours and geographic isolation imply a third trait of night spots — the threat of physical danger. The menace of physical abuse is not an idle one. During the summer of 1969, Bobby W. cruised Central Park on a "typical" evening. He made an urgent pass at an apparently "available" number. Within seconds, Bobby writhed on the ground in pain, his hands frantically trying to stop the bleeding and pain from multiple stab wounds in the abdomen, neck, and face. He was also beaten. Nothing stolen, Bobby concluded that the "freak" was a fag-hater — playing the game of fag-baiting. In another case, two men were murdered in their apartment after taking a pair of laborers home from a Brooklyn park one late summer evening. The workers knew enough of the game to be picked up by the unsuspecting gays. After breaking the neck of one man, and stabbing the other in the back, they made off with a couple of bankbooks, the cashing of which eventually led to their arrest.

Night spots are well known by the police.[2] The police visit a popular Brooklyn park every night around 11:30 p.m. The erotic population, integrating the expected visit into the routine of doing park work on a typical night, assume "covering" tactics as the time of the visit draws near. They desert the bushes and take seats on benches running parallel to a row of hedges. Some quit the park altogether until the coast is clear.

A criminal element certainly knows popular night spots. Andy C., for example, spent all night at the pier one autumn evening. He was "jostled" (pocket picked), losing money and a fine, leather wallet. The observer cautioned Andy to put his money in his shoes and carry no wallet. He did so for the next visit but forgot not to wear a watch. On entering the building, he suddenly remembered he was wearing it and quickly shoved it into a front pocket of his trousers. When he left for home the following morning, the watch was gone. By the way, these losses are sustained during the usual course of sexual events. Someone involved in the sexual scene is also interested in enhancing his material condition.

Theft is a common occurrence at the trucks where it is so dark that touch and subtle noise are the only means of negotiating a liaison. Robbery also takes place in parks. Dr. E took a vacation in P-town. On the evening of arrival, he hurried to the park surrounding the monument, a notorious landmark of nocturnal adventure. He returned to his hotel room without a wallet and the contents of $25 and ten credit cards. He had had a similar experience in a New York City park only ten days before.

Lastly, although some peripheral urban settings (e.g., the park) are legitimate public spaces accessible to all, the use of the space's implicit legitimating aura during crises is precluded because of the inappropriate time of attendance. In fact, city codes often close parks after a certain hour for safety reasons, transforming them into illicit territories during nighttime hours. Privately owned, the trucks and pier require illegal trespass for utilization. Only sporadically visited by the police, their availability encourages heavy community use.

Nocturnal visitations grant easy access to homosexual others but readily attract an unsavory and dangerous element who, because of the circumstances, can pursue their own ends with relative impunity. How can the homosexual manage to evade the real and ever-present threat of danger during nocturnal visits?

THE ROUTINIZATION OF DANGER

Avoiding dangerous situations is a major solution in preventing calamity. It seems contradictory or almost ludicrous to suggest it because the homosexual places himself in the direct line of fire with each visit. Yet, it is widely exercised.

Regulars of nocturnal visits are able to decipher the cues and clues of "typicality" to a given scene, based on previous individual experience and a shared knowledge of it generated by wide community use. The setting must conform to accepted definitions of "typicality" before the nocturnal visitor penetrates a setting's perimeter. These assessments are made during the approach to the setting, the results of which either encourage or dissuade the continuation of the journey to the erotic destination. Readings for conformance may seem a mysterious, intuitive process but certain visible signs of danger do exist for the knowledgeable eye and ear. In examining a park setting, for example, no unusual noise should be emanating from it. The music of drum combos or blasting radios signify the presence of lower class youth. No one enters the park on such a night. The park is also scanned for unusual lights. Is the police patrol car cruising up and down the tree-enshrouded lanes? Flashlights? Fires?

An incident occurred to the observer that nicely outlines the contours of a "typical" night in the park. The observer had wandered over to a Brooklyn park about 11:30 p.m. on a particularly hot and humid evening.[3] The park should have been erotically active by this hour. However, the observer indifferently noticed that it was comparatively empty. Without bothering to ascertain the reasons for the emptiness, he walked along a depression in the earth that meanders along the dark side of a tall row of hedge, looking for action. He paused for a moment to look back at what he thought to be an unfolding dialogue. At that moment, a young man walked over to him and said, "Sir, do you have a dime?"

The inquirer was a young black teenager who, upon rejection, went back through the hedges. Anxiety swept over the observer. He had failed to note that the only individuals in the park at this time were black youths. Two or three older black men were present but not located near the teenagers. The youths were clustered in groups, another danger sign in park settings. The absence of whites who usually frequent this particular park in large numbers presaged even more danger. Something may have happened earlier that prompted their departure. Furthermore, speech, especially in the form of panhandling and gratuitous civility ("Sir") do not occur in erotic settings.

Danger loomed very large. The observer decided to rush for the lighter side of the hedges. At that instant, the youth with several companions rapidly headed his way. With quickening pace, the observer plunged through the foliage and hurriedly walked to the intersecting road. He did not run. He wanted to avoid drawing attention from other nearby groups. The observer headed directly toward clusters of older individuals quietly conversing on the pavement next to the street. Turning around to see if the escape was successful, the observer was relieved to see the youths giving up the chase. Before reaching the group of conversing individuals, the observer heard one pursuer exclaim, "Goddamn, he got away."

The incident underscores the extreme danger of nocturnal sojourns. The public eroticist must deftly "read" and interpret ambiguous cues if he is not only to enjoy sexual ventures but stay alive. The naivete of the observer during this episode highlights the perspicacity of regular attenders who foresaw the danger and abstained from any involvement for the evening.

The congestion of regular attenders at the trucks limits this type of abuse. However, the darkness of the setting encourages jostling and other forms of robbery. The same is true for pier work. The only preventative is leaving valuables at home. Both settings however are located in isolated areas of the city. Physical abuse stalks the journey to and from them. A man from New Jersey was stabbed in his arm (the thrust was toward the neck) as he walked home after spending many hours in the trucks. The victim noticed the youths ahead of him but did not suspect foul intentions. The stabbing took place at about 3:00 a.m. on a deserted street a few blocks from the trucks. Uninterested in material gain the youths seemed to attack for the pleasure of physical abuse. The incident frightened the New Jersey man but has not deterred him from subsequent truck adventures. In fact, he has equipped himself with a cane, weighted with several pounds of copper wire which he intends to use during the next assault.

INITIAL COMMENTS ON CRUISING ATTIRE

Clothing for leisure hour cruising is free of constraints of conventional dress codes. Unless traveling in a car, however, dress cannot exceed certain general societal expectations if the individual is to walk along the street or ride mass transit without embarrassment or ridicule. The significance of special cruising attire in erotic communications is crucial in bar work and will be discussed in detail in the next chapter.

For most nocturnal cruising, there is no special "erotic" attire. Many people wear dark colored clothing to fit in with the shadows of darkness. They have little impact on gestural communications. Others wear white trousers, especially in the summer, which are form-fitting. Blatantly outlining the genitals, they induce erotic interest and sometimes quicken the pace of sexual exchanges.

Whereas those who wear dark clothing do so for added protection, those who wear white do so to be seen. They are not interested in attracting the attention of police, muggers, or criminal elements, of course, but they do hope to be noticed by all those interested in erotic activity.

Those who want to "make out" conform to some degree to general standards of appropriate attire expected at night spots. A middle-aged man, about six feet tall with a protruding stomach, created much consternation for example by appearing in the hedges of a park in a suit and tie. The outfit was entirely anomalous to the attire expectations of the park setting. With his approach individuals within the hedges engaging in sex hurriedly vacated the brush. Sitting on nearby park benches, or journeying over to an adjacent park, they decided that the individual was strange enough to be an impostor. They waited over an hour until the visitor "got the message" that nothing was going to happen until he withdrew. After he did so, the park settled down into a routine evening of activity.

Credentials for erotic acceptance do not depend on specific dress on nocturnal turf as long as it conforms to leisure modes of attire. These standards are affected by current fashion trends and fads. The "flower era" of filmy, colorful attire of the late 1960s has been replaced by the masculine western look of the 70s —moustache, beard, close-cropped hair, plaid shirt, tight jeans, and some form of boot wear.

Individuals who identify with a "fem" or "butch" imagery or who hope to solicit specific sexual practices wear clothing or accessories that cue others in as to how they see themselves and how they think others should see them. Only a few western and leather attired "numbers" have been observed in the parks although that attire is the expected costume at the trucks and pier. A youthful exception, however, regularly attended an oft-observed Brooklyn park. He always wore tight jeans and a leather jacket, no matter how hot the evening. His sexual speciality was "rimming."[4] As the other participants busied themselves with oral sodomy, he would try to pry into the dialogue to rim one or both of the participants if they allowed him to do so. Because wearing leather is associated with exotic sexual practices, the observer can only conclude that the youth's costume was an attempt to broadcast his sexual proclivities.

"GETTING IT ON": ARRANGING NOCTURNAL MATCHES THROUGH GESTURAL NEGOTIATIONS

After the entrant makes a general survey of the park, he decides whether to remain or travel elsewhere. If he decides to stay, his first concern is to discern the identity of an attractive object who has caught his eye — is he safe? Next, does the individual share a reciprocal interest in him? A cautious reading will circumvent the private pain and public humiliation of a rejection. Thirdly, there is the problem of preventing interference from undesirable others. Steeled by continuous neglect, they are dauntless in intruding.

Because the nocturnal visitor is never sure if the object of interest is really out for erotic "kicks" or monetary gain, his attire, physical cleanliness, and attitude are carefully observed and analyzed before serious cruising cues are dropped. Shoddy, unkempt clothing, body odor, and an inability to fit into the behavior patterns of silent discourse during a "typical" night in the park portend a suspicious identity.

Anyone reacting to initial overtures in a peculiar way, not responding at all, or negatively overreacting, creates distrust. As an example, a white male, about 28 years old, walked past a neatly and casually attired black leaning against an iron fence found on the periphery of the park. The white guy found him attractive. He signaled interest by walking past him a second time within a few minutes. A brief but intense stare accompanied the second sweep. The black man simply looked down at the pavement, with hands grasping the fence on each side of his body. Acting bolder, the white male assumed a leaning position on the fence, not more than four feet from the black man — an incontrovertible display of interest. The latter continued his preoccupation with the pavement. The white male continued glancing toward him with increasingly frequent stares. Finally, the black male looked over at the white guy with a fierce look in his eyes and then returned to his detached singularity. Within seconds, the latter had walked out of the park.

Initial cues of interest include walking past the object more than once, with or without glancing at him; briefly looking at someone who has walked past, either once or twice; turning the head in the direction of a passing individual, particularly if he turns around after passing; the use of propinquity by placing oneself near enough to the object to indicate interest but distant enough to withdraw quickly if the individual is hostile or nonresponsive; and perhaps making the most dramatic gesture of availability — not directed to any one individual but to the park population in general, at least those of whom are watching — the disappearance into one of the "meat rack" areas. Following an individual after a walk-by is also an indication of interest although it sometimes generates fear in the followed.

Impatience occasionally dictates remarkably obvious

displays. One middle-aged man, having evoked no response from the usual repertoire of cues, sauntered over to a path in a nearby row of tall hedges, pulled out his penis, and massaged it into an erection. Standing sideways, the light shining from the opposite direction silhouetted the erection. He motioned to an individual standing near a bench to follow. The strategem worked. Both disappeared into the hedges.

If a response is gleaned from the behavior of an interesting object, or if the participant believes he saw a response, additional cues are unleashed to encourage the growth of a dialogue. If posturing takes place anywhere other than in a protected area that camouflages direct sexual contact the liaison must be deepened to an extent that will persuade both respondents to seek a sheltered area in which sex can take place. Arranging a nocturnal match, however, is an ever-creative process as the following example illustrates.

During an observation in an autumn evening, at about 11:30 p.m. a man in his late twenties, hereafter known as Mr. X, dressed in jeans, sat on one of the benches in a small sparsely planted park. A thin tree grows some ten feet from the bench, the only foliage within a 25 foot radius. Mr. X spotted Mr. Z as the latter entered the park some 50 feet away. He stared as Mr. Z gradually descended toward his direction. Mr. Z was a Hispanic-looking man in his late 30s, also dressed in jeans and teeshirt. As he entered the park, his eyes thoroughly surveyed the environs as he walked. Nearing the bench of Mr. X, he looked the latter's way but continued looking around the park. Mr. Z passed the bench to some distance. During this time, Mr. X followed him with his eyes, the head turning in pursuit of Mr. Z's travels. The rest of the park was quiet. Mr. Z finally stopped and reversed his course. On the way back, he began looking at Mr. X from some distance. The latter returned the stares. As Z neared the bench, each held the other in long visual embraces. Z passed the bench by a few feet, stopped, turned to look at X once again, and found the latter still staring. Z returned to the bench and sat down two feet from X. A series of brief looks passed between the couple.

Finally, Z touched his groin. X followed the example. To the surprise of the observer who stood only ten feet behind the bench on a rise of the ground, the two did not repair to one of the meat racks to complete the episode. Noting that several people had entered the bushy area just prior to their meeting who might interfere should they relocate there, the pair remained seated on the openly visible bench. Mr. Z pulled out his penis and massaged it. Mr. X did the same. Mr. Z fondled Mr. X's penis. Mr. X bent over and fellated Z. He did not stop until Z had an orgasm. After he did so, Z closed his trousers, tapped X on the shoulder in a gesture of thanks, and departed. X got up and walked into the large meat rack for additional activity.

THE "UNCEREMONIOUS" MEAT RACK

Meat rack areas are customary regions in public parks. As designated, protected ecological niches they encompass specific territory such as the large clump of bushes centered in an active, downtown Brooklyn park.

Meat rack participation does not require much if any gesturing before touching. A tacit agreement exists whereby access to one's physical being is openly permitted. Refusals are equally abrupt and without ceremony. All meat racks share this implicit understanding, from the daylight bird sanctuary at T____ Beach, to the ink-black forests utilized by Fire Islanders at night.

For example, the aforementioned Mr. X who was observed disappearing into the meat rack of the downtown Brooklyn park was quickly followed by the observer. Upon pushing through the bushes, a middle-aged man grabbed for X's cock. X caught his wrist and shoved it aside. Without stopping to recover himself, the man lunged toward the observer who deftly sidestepped him. Refused twice, he left.

The observer, Mr. X, another middle-aged man, and two youths stood face-to-face within the small, dimly lit leafy enclosure. The two young men reached out and fondled one another without regard for the others present, obviously resuming a transaction that our arrival interrupted. One pinched the other's nipples, while the latter concentrated energies on the penis. Grabbing each other, they kissed vigorously, grinding pelvises together.

X walked over to them and without forewarning touched the buttocks of each. They parted slightly, looked at X, and gradually absorbed him into the action. The two youths opened each other's trousers and pulled out respective cocks. They turned to X and did the same. X grabbed both penes. Meanwhile, the older man had commenced rubbing his penis through the trousers. His head turned inquisitively toward the observer who, anticipating a "rush," maintained a studious visual involvement with the evolving threesome to cue the middle-aged man that he was not interested. However, the man slowly inched his way around the narrow area so that he stood within touching distance of the observer. From the corner of his eye, the observer noticed the guy's hand slowly reaching for his groin. Equally paced, the observer cupped his genitals with the hands. The man "read" the message and transferred his attention to the threesome. Rather than close in on them immediately, he moved to about 18 inches from one youth. He pulled out a large penis and stood motionless, masturbating. He waited to be seen by one of the three. By this time, however, they were too engrossed to notice, alternating between fellatio and kissing. X pulled one youth's pants down to the knees and tried to penetrate the anus with his penis while the other youth fellated him. Receiving little notice, the older man closed in on the side of X and thrust his penis into X's hand. X grabbed it, turned toward the older man, squatted on his knees and lustily fellated him. Noting that orgasm would no doubt conclude this four-cornered arrangement, the observer terminated his observation.

NOTES

1. Night spots are an integral part of the "secret" subcultural gay world requiring leisure hours for participation. See Warren, 1974: 45–49.
2. See "Parks, tearoom hot spots," *The Advocate,* 4:13, 1970: 3.
3. The weather is an important factor in this episode. Escaping the heat of ghetto walls and streets, bands of youths migrated from usual territory and headed for the closest open space that promised some air. They arrived at the park in remarkably large numbers. Dispersing throughout the park in groups, their numbers remained inconspicuous.
4. "Rimming" is the sexual practice of licking the anus with the tongue and/or sucking on it with the mouth.

chapter 6

"The Manneristic" Worlds of the Gay Bar and Pig Parlor

COMMON PROPERTIES OF SHELTERED SETTINGS

Gay bars, pig parlors, and gay baths are owned and operated by private entrepreneurs expressly for the enjoyment of homosexuals. Not only unwelcome, heterosexuals are systematically discouraged from any patronage. Should they accidentally stumble into a gay establishment, the all-male population, and the setting's decorative motif precipitates a fast-developed self-consciousness and a strong desire for immediate withdrawal. If the unwanted patron remains, the bartender may refuse to serve him or management may simply ask him or her to leave the premises.

Past and current pig parlors are organized as private clubs. Entrance is by

membership only, which prevents accidental intrusion. Gay baths control attendance by carefully scrutinizing those seeking admission. Suspicious faces are asked if they have been on the premises before. If answers seem inappropriate or if suspicion persists, the cashier will state outright that the bath is only for homosexuals or explain that the bath is filled to capacity.

Bar, pig-parlor, and bath settings therefore do not function to sift out heterosexuals or imposters. It is taken for granted that this is done at the door. Their primary purposes are to create an acceptable atmosphere for posturing erotic statements, facilitate communications between patrons, and process erotic overtures and possible outcomes without destroying the credibility of patrons or disturbing the flow of interaction in the setting.

Given the protective nature of sheltered environments, the door to anxiety about conventional concerns slams shut for the homosexual. The fear of possible coercion and social abuse fast recedes into the far depths of background concerns, no longer figuring in identity management and social interaction.

Defined as total homosexual situations, sheltered settings are devoted only to homosexual interests and pursuits. Usually segregated in time and space from heterosexual routines, the homosexual discards his straight identities with a feeling of security. Subcultural gear is dragged out of the closet.

We enter then a comprehensively erotic world. Functioning on a 24-hour schedule, it forms an ever-present shadow world behind that of the conventional one. Whenever at leisure, before, between, or after conventional pursuits, the individual knows that a totally homosexual environment awaits him. However, the world of sheltered settings does have a temporal rythm based on its intimate relationship to conventional demands, that mark the peak and ebb of community participation. This will be discussed below.

Going "public" before a totally homosexual audience radically transforms the host of routinely attendant matters to which the individual must attend if he is to be accepted in subcultural situations. The threads of interaction in this world are woven into an all-embracing frame, which has its own idiosyncratic organization, mores, manners, and conventions.

EXPECTATIONAL HORIZONS OF BAR AND PIG PARLOR SETTINGS

Bars attract specific clientele because the clientele believes the bar to attract this clientele. The patron identifies with the imagery, behavior, attitudes, mannerisms, attire, and sexual practices ascribed to this clientele. These beliefs constitute the symbolic and intentional contours and hence expectations and anticipations of the bar and of those who attend it.

As a physical and symbolic setting, the bar and pig parlor cater to the reputation acquired from its clientele or to one that it has been trying to establish. By decorative motifs, attire of bartenders, and type of music, an intentional atmosphere is created that sustains the various typified identities expected to be found there. Ty's rustic interior of crude brick wall, old-fashioned western bar, wagon wheels, and blaring, stomping music, for example, fosters a "range-type" of atmosphere. The 1950s records on the jukebox, elegant red velvet wallpaper, crystal sconces, barmaid, and refined bar generate a staid gentlemanly ambiance in the Coat of Arms. The sexual objectives of the situation are, of course, suggested in the total combination of setting features because they are associated with the patron's maximally gratifying sexual object.

The symbolic and intentional atmosphere of the bar functions as a screening device by which mutually attractive identities can meet in a routine setting — a setting conducive to a taken-for-grantedness and, at the same time, be a real and symbolic buttressing of homosexual identity. Individuals who identify themselves and others as belonging to a type of setting feel an attraction to a particular location. In a circular sense, those who posture certain identities and attend a particular bar setting expecting to find similar identities there generate the reputational and self-fulfilling aspects of the bar. The symbolic suggestiveness of the setting dictate the various appropriate pegs, cues, and other indices to wear to comply with the expectations of the identifying nexus. The success with which the indices are exhibited determines the patron's position on the continuum of desirability.

Setting modalities play an important part in sustaining the patron's identity in the only area of social life that routinely accepts his self-statements as a homosexual. The heavily attired leather participant, bedecked from head to foot in black leather, metal studs, and chains, feels absolutely secure, "normal" in the Eagle, Spike, Kellers, Zodiac, or Choo-Choos. The individual is not only able to express who he "really" is but receives vital recognition and support in this expression. His conception of self is buttressed by others who are busy making similar identity statements and claims. This mirroring effect and the positive if indirect reactions from others form a mutual bond of identity support and conviction.

Identity modalities and typifications contribute to the mobilization of erotic interest. These identities comprise the sexual universe of the individual. Associations to the texture of cloth, imagery of attire, mannerisms, attitudes, and personal styles, circumscribed by the symbolic nuances of the setting, escalate the patron into an erotic frame of reference. Denim, suede, or leather, worn tight around the human frame, accentuating physical aspects of the body, particularly the groin, are focal points of attention.

Normative pressures push the patron toward conformance in self-presentations and performances. They must conform to the clientele's expectations. The patron is noticed and interacted with if he meets these expectations. The Eagle, a leather bar, for example, rewards those who wear leather by reducing the price of a drink (on certain nights) or bestows special attention in the form of a "drink on the house." Management prohibits entrance to those who wear sandals, shorts, or striped shirts.

Bars then attract typified identities — especially in large metropolitan areas where large populations of homosexuals support specializing staging establishments. Boston, Chicago, San Francisco, and Washington, D.C., to name a few of many cities, have special bars that include western, leather, S-M, dance, and "piss-elegant" bars.[1] When the patron decides to go to a bar, he makes a conscious statement as to which population with whom he choses to identify. He expects to find this population at the chosen bar. The piss-elegant patron does not expect leather people at his bar. Both consider the presence of the other ludicrous. Communications and interaction are seriously impeded by the appearance of incongruous identities. After all, the patron wishes to socialize with individuals with whom he can interact and relate to in a comfortable, taken-for-granted way.

Management of an establishment often engage in supportive practices to encourage the attendance of the correct and expected crowd. The back room of the original Stud at one time was off limits to those not dressed in leather or suede. The Coat of Arms absolutely required patrons to wear a suit and tie. Without them, entrance was blocked by a "bouncer." The more stylized the costume, the more out of the way the location of the setting, unless the style conformed to conventional dress. Leather bars are usually located along the isolated dark docks of the city. Settings peopled by less costumed types are found on major avenues of the city, usually behind acceptable facades. Regents Row, for example, another piss-elegant establishment, is located in a posh area of the city noted for its stable businesses and wealthy residents.

Not all bars are rigidly typed. A bar in "P," New Hampshire, the only gay bar within a large geographical area is patronized by a wide spectrum of erotic identities. Clusters of leather, collegiate, fluffy sweater, and nellies hang together. Communication and interaction patterns separate the groups that tend to cruise within their identity group.

There is an alienative factor in the bar, as in almost all other erotic silent settings, relating to identity typifications. Interaction and social relations devolve on the constellation of identity equipment and imagery captured by the moment rather than presented by the "person." That is, any person — not simply this unique individual — is related to if appropriate use has been made of his sign equipment, imagery, cues, and behavior. Denim, leather belt and boots, and bare hairy chest, for example, are the foci of attention during social interaction rather than the biographical individual who wears them (all of this depends on the congruity of the individual's mannerisms and presentation with his garb). Participants do not speak to each other, unless with consociates, because the quality of the voice, and the nature of the vocabulary of everyday conversation destroy erotic portrayals. As H.G. so often states, "I don't want them to talk; it ruins the image."

On the other hand, stylized identities and presentations represent a universalistic quality that contributes to easy communication and interaction. Again focusing on the leather individual, the New Yorker will feel perfectly at ease in San Francisco, Montreal, Boston, Toronto, Cologne, Munich, and London, because all have settings that call for leather drag and presentations. During the summer of 1974, a chartered flight from West Germany of over 300 leathermen arrived in New York City for an informal, international leather convocation at Cherry Grove. For one week, more German than English could be overheard in the community. Language barriers did not exist between the leather individuals. Attire, stylized portraits, and material cues communicated identities and roles.

The same may be noted about the piss-elegant world. From the Napoleon in Boston and the Yukon in New York City, to Die Stadt in Hamburg and the Zanzibar in Munich, the patron knows that attire expectations demand a suit and tie, or its equivalent. The setting is one of plushness and quiet background music. The norms of piss-elegance prohibit "gross" gestural communications such as displaying erections or rubbing groins. A token purchase of a drink, mediated by the waiter or bartender, initiates a hoped-for liaison. A rejection is carefully blunted by the mediator so that an unwanted overture creates little notice and embarrassment. With the acceptance of a drink, the bartender informs the recipient of who sent the drink. A nod is usually exchanged between parties, which might eventually lead to a conversation.

INTERIOR PROPS TO EROTIC PORTRAYALS

Names of bars frequently suggest a "typified" identity. The Eagle, Ramrod, Spike, Boot Hill, Roadhouse, and Ty's imply a firm, masculine imagery, stressing western to leather gear; the Candy Store, Coat of Arms, and Regents Row, the piss-elegant set; and Piano Bar and Goldbug, the drag and dance set.

Light is universally dark in bar settings except those that present a nongay facade due to windows directly accessible to outside viewing, e.g.; Julius' Bar. Subtle light enhances the "virtual" appearance of the individual. Red and orange light seem the standard interior hue. Heavy layers of smoke also help blur the hard lines of physical appearances.

The stand-up, cruising bar is Spartanly equipped. Aside from the stools surrounding the bar, the ubiquitous and necessary jukebox,[2] an occasional pool table, the cigarette machine, and the toilet, the only other decorations are accessories that make some kind of identity statement about the population of the bar.

Physical aspects of the bar focus attention on cruising. Spacious empty areas not only accommodate large numbers of patrons, but permit enough "runway" space to allow the continual flow of individuals to incessantly ply back and forth among the crowd, exhibiting and posturing physical virtues while searching for the desired, erotic object of the evening. In a popular bar such as Kellers, for example, the pool table is covered on weekends to conserve desperately needed space. It also adds another surface on which to lean (and posture). A narrow bar at best, Kellers becomes so crowded that even getting inside the bar is difficult. Bodies mash tightly against each other, encouraging touch even if by accident. Squeezing through the throng, touching as one goes, is a crucial input in Kellers' popularity. The compactness of the bar and the fact that the patron is physically pressed against several other men generate sensuousness and a feeling of belonging, in spite of a lack of verbal intercourse.

With the exception of a few bar stools, the bar and pig parlor have no sit down facilities except window ledges. The lack of tables and chairs is not an oversight in interior decoration. Standing positions afford full view of potentialities and permit easy movement back and forth. They also provide accessibility between interested parties. For example, leaning against the jukebox is a favorite position. Not only is it a focal point of bar activity (a continual stream of patrons journey back and forth to   it to play favorite songs), but it also permits easy access to an individual leaning against it without making an obvious, direct approach that an isolated position requires. Posturing and self-exhibition generate a constant drift between the various locations in the setting. Obstructions are kept to a minimum so as not to interfere with this steady stream of movement.

THE PARLANCE OF CLOTHING

Identity typifications demand visible imagery to be appropriate. They consist of a complex mix of somatic features, clothing, self-presentations, and performances. "Virtual" identity is reciprocally established by the mirroring effect of similarly typified individuals within a compatible setting.

The patron views his participation and acceptance as an important form of identity legitimation. Rejection is not only socially disruptive but psychologically painful. The idea is to be accepted as one of the crowd. Clothing contributes significantly to acceptance, encourages sociation, and reinforces the belief in one's identity. For example, Ty's attracts a youthful western set. That is, those in attendance wear jeans, a western type of shirt, usually plaid in design, some type of boot gear, and accents that fit into a "cowboy-type" attire; e.g., cowboy hat, handkerchief (red, blue, or yellow) dangling from a rear trouser pocket, and leather wrist band.[3] Kellers' clientele is also outfitted in jeans, western shirt and boots. Most patrons sport moustache, beard, or both. The teeshirt, jeans, leather belt, boots, and accessories are assumed to reflect the person in the casualness and perfectly natural attitude of the masculine person.

Attending a bar without wearing the appropriate attire is a waste of effort and often embarrassing. The older patron, for example, who showed up one night in shirt and slacks at the Stud was greeted with incredulous smiles and careful neglect. He hung on till the bitter end, pretending not to notice the indifference, nay avoidance, that pursued him from room to room.

The fact that similar identity pegs monopolize a setting makes "standing out" in the crowd a problem. Clothing and personal styles of coming across (performances) become very important in identity portrayals and projections, and the responses they elicit. Given the range of attire, personal accouterment in jewelry, hair styles, hats and handkerchiefs, and self-presentational styles, the patron must be able not only to sustain situational expectations but in addition, and without distressing protocol, be different in some way to attract attention. To claim attention, individuals accent costumes with large hats of various textures and exotic boots with spurs, or wear totally extreme accessories such as leather chaps without under garments. One youth, for example, noted for his muscular chest, wears nothing to cover it up when attending bars, even in freezing weather. Those with large genitals inevitably gain attention and enhance status by baldly displaying carefully arranged "cocks and balls." A black patron in his early thirties, for example, stood at the bar of the Spike one warm, summer evening. He wore a tattered western shirt with sleeves rolled up above the elbows. He had carefully arranged on the right thigh what appeared to be a massive penis. The tight jeans hugged each and every curve of the flesh.

Wearing no underwear, the trousers around the buttocks appeared "tucked" into the crevice of the anal region. Amazing to the observer, however, and to everyone at the bar, was a tear in the trouser's right thigh exactly where the glans of the penis reclined. Due to the light in the bar, one could not determine if the head of the penis was in or out of the trousers. This was an exceptionally clever staging device. Aside from the fact that he exhibited the large penis, always a strong beacon for attention, the confusion as to whether it was in or out of the trousers, and the interest that the puzzle aroused, drew a great deal of visual comment during the period of time the patron spent in the bar. The man remained at the bar for an hour, not changing positions so that the interesting features of his costume would be duly seen and appreciated by everyone. (He was noted to leave alone an hour after he had made his entrance.)

Extreme identities cannot go through the streets in full regalia without receiving undue debilitating notice, even ridicule. They travel by cab or private car. Only on isolated Fire Island can the submissive "M" be entirely chained, hooded without sight, and led around on a leash like a dog (observation, summer 1970).

PERSUASIVE DEPORTMENT

Deportment is as crucial as wearing correct attire. Performances reinforce the patron's "virtual" identity if they match the impression his attire creates. To do so requires minute attention to the complex variables of coming across "correctly," e.g., controlling posture, interest or lack of interest in those around him, body movement, obvious nervousness, and other kinetic manifestations. All are tied into the axes of identity imputations by others and the expectations to which they give rise.

Number 9, for example, towers above the crowd[4]. A six-foot youth of about 25 years of age, he dresses only in jeans, teeshirt (white), and boots. The teeshirt bulges with a well-developed chest and torso. Legs appear massive under the jeans. His waist is amazingly narrow. The physical appearance of Number 9 attracts a great deal of attention and, if he is not careful, many erotic overtures. When walking or pushing through a bar throng, Number 9 maintains an air of patient nonchalance. He seems unable to see others around him, although his air is not one of total indifference. His gaze, always forward, precedes a panther-like body movement. At no time does he look from patron to patron. After securing a position, the face remains calm, composed, not unfriendly, but not inviting. He reacts like a picture in a gallery; hung to be seen, observed, and admired, but something that does not react back to the admirer. Demeanor is carefully masculine. No movement is made that does not contribute to image maintenance. Unlike other patrons in the bar, no attention is given to maintaining a given level of grooming. He does not touch the hair, pick his nails, or peer in the mirror or window to perfect a nuance of irregularity. Projecting an image of perfect composure and total inner security, the mystery of Number 9 has created a large following of admirers.

Body idiom confirms and reaffirms what the patron asks others to believe of his image. The way he holds a bottle of beer — with a full hand rather than by a few fingers — and the casual way he observes others around him are carefully attended to lest some item of behavior cast suspicion on the identity he presents. Don P., for instance, wears "shades" to the Eagle to create a severe, tough look, and to veil interest in others. If found actively cruising, his image as a strong "S" would be threatened. The "S" does not have to cruise.

A careful balance of acute and casual interest in others is meticulously blended if the patron is not to be imputed as either snobby and lost to "role play" or too hungry for consideration. If he moves from one spot to another permitting exposure to the entire diversity of patrons, he maintains a casual air, making sure that his gait or stride and the way he moves the body enhance or at least sustain the identity impression he makes through attire and attitude. In one instance, a lanky six-footer, handsome and with a large penis could not understand why he was not receiving overtures in bars. He did a self-appraisal before a mirror, changing attire, style of walk, and manner of smiling. He adopted a western image and began attending western bars. He learned to move slowly, the stride an additional testament to his "masculinity." He noted an immediate and gratifying improvement in attention (from a letter sent by John A. of San Francisco, 1971).

Status is seriously threatened if the patron falls out of role. An accidental "swish" in a butch or leather bar, confrontation by screaming "fem sisters," and other unanticipated events either crush status claims or seriously imperil them. Consociate approaches usually terminate erotic dialogues. Erotic maneuvering must be put aside, at least temporarily, to sociate on a nonerotic level. When Don E. and the observer entered the Eagle or Spike together, it was understood that the observer was to drift off so that Don could "do his thing."

THE STUD

In early 1969, Dr. E excitedly reported to the observer that a new bar opened in the village. It was a western leather bar. Consisting of two rooms, a regular bar set-up occupied one room. Entrance to the other room reportedly required suede, denim, or leather attire. Rumors were rife that sexual activity took place in the second room. Because the observer had minimal exposure to western/leather bars at the time, having sporadically observed only Dirty Dicks and Kellers during a few week nights that proved uninteresting (due to a lack of customers), the observer wanted to go immediately. The following Tuesday was the introductory night of observation. The bar was consistently observed at least once a week thereafter. Observation lasted almost the entire "first" three-year career of the bar.

The Stud is located on "G" Street in the warehouse section of the West Village, an area notorious for esoteric settings and erotic activities. Blocks from the heavy tourist section of the Village, little residential traffic travels these streets. The area is a favorite site for homosexual bars.

The Stud caters to a "butch" crowd. That is what the bar is all about. Mannerisms, self-presentations, and performances are carefully tailored and continually policed to remain with the frame of expectations of the masculine individual. Attention to the minutest detail, such as the way one holds a cigarette,[5] constantly preoccupies consciousness.

The main room, the one immediately accessible from the street, is entered through a door located in the corner of the room opposite the bar. Patrons already present usually stand along the sides of each of the plate glass walls that meet it, forming a human corridor through which each new arrival passes to make his initial survey of the setting and/or get to the bar and adjacent back room. From the moment of arrival, the individual is appraised. The mere sound of the opening door is a magnet for inquiring eyes.

Careful attention to performance commences upon the patron's entrance to the bar. Because great expectations exist in bar work — Mr. Ideal's entrance is momentarily expected — acute attention welcomes new arrivals. Knowing that he will be observed immediately, the new entrant must establish a credible identity as soon as he steps foot in the bar. Yet, in spite of debut pressures, the patron must somehow appear casual, at ease, "himself," in the appropriate attire and attitude. Not infrequently, an accidental and embarrassing trip of the foot, caused by the concentration on being "casual" rather than on where one walks, temporarily mars the carefully maintained casualness.

No one breaks from his carefully poised posture while looking at the new entrant. Heads turn slightly while eyes strain to see. Bodies continue the quiet gyration to the music pouring out of the jukebox. Patrons studiously avoid hard stares.[6] Strong visual thrusts appear "hungry," creating an image of too-hungry-for-some-reason-and-thus-to-be-avoided-for-same-unknown-reason.

After securing a position for posturing, the patron begins

the evening's activities. He is both director and recipient of a polyphony of interests. Choice in bar placement is crucial not only for purposes of accessibility, but for the display of what he thinks are his assets. If, for example, he thinks he has large genitals, he positions himself against the wall in such a way that by resting his back on the wall in a concave position, the penis and testes will be thrust up, accentuating their size. A recent emigre from Israel, for instance, chose to sit on a chair for his best presentations at the Blue Whale on Fire Island. He sat on its edge, legs spread far apart, pushing the back of the chair against the wall in a leaning position. Thrust up for all to see was a large groin bulge. Carefully detailed in tight-fitting jeans it was projected outward so that it could not be missed.

The erotic horizons of sheltered settings are punctuated by stars — the universally desired — and lesser stellar identities. Status is gauged by the "obvious" interest from other patrons. Eye contact, propinquity, and flow of gestural signals, particularly head movement, distinquish the multi-layered indications of attractiveness. A German-born man, for example, handsomely tall and trim, and sporting a large mustache, draws immediate attention the moment he arrives at The Stud. Streams of people flow past to look him over. Heads twist and turn in his direction as he moves from one room to the next.

Those with inappropriate attire, deportment, and apparent physical inferiority elicit negative reactions. Non-involvement encircles them. Occupying dark corners of the bar, they rapidly sally back and forth, accosting any and all patrons with hungry, bold eyes.

The patron radiates interest by self-presentation and carefully monitored eye communication. At the same time, he discourages any overtures from uninteresting others by not looking at them.[7] The calm indifference of Number 9 is one technique by which the individual attempts to control overtures directed at him. As a protective shield from unwanted inquiries, it also bolsters identity imagery by carefully controlling information about himself.

The difficulty with managing these contrapuntal concerns is that, if the patron does not display enough interest, it is interpreted as "conceit."[8] The ever-smiling patron, for example, is considered a sham. Bar work is serious. Smiles are reserved for the last phases of communication.

Signals may be mistakenly received and responded to by patrons other than to whom they are directed. During an evening's observation, for example, the observer carefully concealed his observation of two men involved in a dialogue by turning his head in another direction before either of the pair discovered his gaze. While averting their eye contact, his line of vision was unconsciously directed to a man in his late twenties, dressed entirely in western gear, who happened to be standing near the couple. The observer had duly noted him when initially assuming a position against the wall, but the unfolding dialogue had entirely preoccupied his attention. As the observer looked back and forth, the patron apparently interpreted the brief glances as visual overtures. The observer was suddenly shocked to find this individual standing squarely in front of him (one of the few direct approaches involving voice encountered by the observer) saying, "Do you like three-ways?" Recovering quickly but with obvious embarrassment, the observer fumbled, "What do you mean?"

"I have a friend at home, just below Hudson. Looks something like me. Do you like to get fucked by a big cock?" he continued. The observer floundered and wondered what to say next, realizing the "obvious" commitment the patron made when venturing over. The observer reflected for a moment and then replied, "Sounds great. But I don't get involved with anyone I haven't seen first." The patron seemed satisfied with the reply. He smiled, and moved onto the next room. When the observer left the bar about a half hour later, he observed the man engaged in conversation in a rear corner.

Before signaling any interest to an interesting individual, the patron secures a position opposite from him. This placement provides easy visual range of the person. Standing opposite the interesting individual, casually smoking and drinking, the patron follows the path of the individual's visual inquiries, mentally noting those with whom he communicates. He can gauge the probability of engaging the individual in a dialogue by noting the types he looks at. The patron may give up at this point and relocate if he sees little likelihood of success. Number 9 and the German, for instance, never seem to be looking anywhere. Their imposing physical presentations defy overtures, or so it seems, and in spite of provoking interest, seem to elicit few propositions. If the patron thinks there is an erotic possibility, he occasionally looks over at the object of interest, trying to engage the eyes in a mutual contact.

Attempting to arrest someone's attention in a small bar packed with 200 people milling back and forth is no easy task, particularly when the other individual is busily engaged in following the constant parade of posturing "numbers." Nevertheless, the patron tries his luck by persistently glancing over. By the way, in spite of initiating overtures, the patron continues looking around, lest he miss a better opportunity.

If initial eye thrusts are successful, the other patron will reciprocate. Thereafter, the patrons exchange glances, longer looks, and then stares, between increasingly brief time intervals. The visual may be accompanied by smiles or a wink of an eye (rarely). The patron heightens the degree of interest by moving next to the other patron.

When propinquity is used in connection with heavy visual discourse, the dialogue has matured to a point that requires either subtle touching of the other patron's body or verbal exchange. Some informants state that they touch the other guy's groin during this period of the ritual and have their groin felt in return. At Kellers, for example, the trousers were opened in one instance and the penis actually pulled out of the trousers. John R. also relates that he had anal intercourse with a patron during a busy evening at Kellers, apparently with little notice from those mashed up against the couple. This type of contact is perfectly acceptable in the bath scene but it is not considered appropriate in bars other than the pig parlor.

When the patron moves next to someone to touch him,

the touch is placed on the arms or legs — a "voluntary" yet accidental touch, not a direct molestation. However, this depends on the type of communications preceding the move, and the type of engrossment each thought the other exhibited before touching commences.

The sudden arrival of an interloper poses a serious threat to an evolving encounter. One evening in the Stud, for instance, the observer was standing next to a rather short, well-built, dark-haired individual who had been engaged in an intense visual dialogue with a rather pale, lanky patron standing along the opposite wall, approximately ten feet away. Both parties were obviously interested in each other. Prolonged and intense stares passed with great frequency between them. Suddenly, the man standing next to the short, black-haired youth turned to him, said something, and then smiled. The attention of the short man was momentarily usurped as he brushed off the overture. However, the lanky man across the way, unable to hear the conversation, noted the shift in attention. Crestfallen, he squeezed his can of beer, "noted it was empty" (one "apparent excuse" to leave an unsuccessful scene and directed to any would-be onlooker), and withdrew to the outside room. Meanwhile, the short patron turned to look for the lanky communicant, but could not find him. His eyes swept the entire room. The observer assumes he thought the lanky man left the bar. He simply resumed the posture of "indifference" and returned to appraising the flowing stream of patrons.

The Stud, like most cruising bars, does not permit sexual activity on its premises. Patrons have to make subsequent arrangements for sexual interaction, which inevitably involves verbal discourse. The difficulty in making the first introductory statement is supreme. Social form up until this point has been entirely visual, gestural, and physical — stuff of conjecture, just short of "fact." The identity of the other patron has been established and sustained by the carefully tailored atmosphere of the bar, and by mutual imputations constructed out of fragile significations. Suppose either of the patrons has a high-pitched voice. Imagery is ruined. The problem then becomes one of withdrawal from an untenable situation if a high-pitched voice is an unacceptable attribute. Furthermore, the erotic mode of communication makes any introductory statement almost irrelevant, taking it out of the context of the moment. Yet, the major question of "Do you want to go home and ball?", the whole point of an evening's cruising, is of central concern but the last to be asked, if at all. To the contrary, introductory statements involve comments on the weather, the crowdedness of the bar, the thickness of the smoke, or if the first person to speak is daring, an introduction to his name.[9] In addition, the "mundaness" of a subway, bus, or taxi ride must be faced if sex is to take place at home. Bright lights illuminate imperfections concealed by the subtle lighting of the bar. The highly sensuous communications of erotic posturing are replaced with trite, perhaps meaningless conversation. Many dialogues collapse for these reasons, laments Dr. P.

The response to the initial statement is equally crucial. If the other patron is hesitant or unresponsive, the aggressive patron gropes for a few more statements before giving up and plunging back into the reserve of bar activity. The other patron may try to string the patron along as he looks for a more interesting partner. If either loses enthusiasm and lapses into silence, an excuse is eventually made, ending the introduction. A comment about purchasing another beer, or noting that it is time to move on, are commonly used excuses. And finally, if the dialogue's ardor endures the verbal introduction, arrangements for subsequent action are made.

The ritual of cautiously placed communications is laborious, taking many hours, and frequently concluding in no contact. The public nature of erotic overtures, and the possibility of visual rejection, together with the fact that the patron is never sure that the object of desire is really interested despite heavy visual work, militate against a more concrete approach to an introduction. Frozen into visual and gestural communications, often so obtuse as to remain obscure, frustration, boredom, and inebriation occur. Patrons often leave the bar for the trucks or parks where sexual encounters are immediate. The cycle of leather bar work in fact is as follows: several hours of serious posturing at the Eagle or Spike (gratifying to identity in a certain sense) punctuated by drinks, and then departure for the trucks or pier where sex takes place quickly. A night of piss-elegant bar participation may terminate in the baths.

If cruising is unsuccessful during the evening, closing hour's pressures bring home the real possibility of leaving alone (a dramatic loss of status). As the hour hurries on, movement throughout the bar increases. Visual dialogues become aggresssive, almost hostile. "Wanting hours" often result in hastily arranged matches, or intensifying levels of tension. All is lost, however, when white lights blaze on and reveal the "nakedness" of the individual. Tired red eyes, haggard from drinking and irritated from smoke, look about at glaring reality. Flooded out, erotic contours collapse. The clientele rapidly fade away.

THE PIG PARLOR: AN OPENLY SEXUAL BAR

On February 20, 1970, Dr. E wrote the following letter:
The Zoo is an after hours bar in the village that opens about midnight. I was there one recent Saturday...And they have liquor, dancing, fuck movies, and a dark room behind the juke box JUST FOR SEX. I 'came' five times between 1:30 a.m. and 6 a.m. In addition to the five who did me, another five or six went down on me. They were all 'stars' by my standards and I was really turned on. I went down on one guy, and he was hung like a horse (another hang up of mine). There are blow jobs going on at the Zodiac too, but these are in the major bar area in the light, and crowded as hell. Both are exciting. I'd much rather take you to these places, than the movies, since those nights are tame by comparison. During the movie the bar is crowded and people grope you. Big Deal. At the other place they 'do' you! Fri and Sat nite would be best. But I suspect the room in the Zoo is used every night, since the owners do not care what you do.

Until January 1966, when a liberal Republican mayor ended an essentially conservative policy toward homosexual settings, including open and frequent harrassment, the bars and few baths that budded on the city's homosexual landscape were controlled by the rackets.[10] The same management could be discerned in the ever-changing gay scene. With liberalization, independent money found its way into the homosexual market, diminishing returns on invested dollars. No longer a high risk industry, illicit money was driven out of the market to some extent. New bars rapidly appeared all over the city, driving down the cost of drinks and profits.

The pig parlor was a new concept in homosexual merchandising, not only squeezing as many services into one area as possible, including drinking, dancing, and sexual activity, but extending the clock of homosexual establishments to a 24-hour basis.[11] Regular bars function until 4:00 a.m. The pig parlor picked up the slack until 8:00 a.m. and even later.

Permitting open sexual activity on the premises revived the illicit nature of the setting, rejuvenating the high risk in the industry. The rackets re-emerged, managing every pig parlor. The erotic back room of course was an absolute requirement in these establishments if the investment was to pay off. Without the novel attraction, the number of competitive settings simply made new investment unprofitable.

The Zoo was the first pig parlor opened in the city, Dr. E states. Eight other "after-hour bars" followed, including the Zodiac, Barn, Peter Pan's Magic Garbage Can, Carnival, and Christopher's End. They catered to specific erotic categories of homosexual types like regular stand-up bars, but differed from the latter in several important ways.

The main difference, of course, was the orgy room where physical sexual activity took place. Other differences included a required membership card for entrance (obtainable only through recommendation of another member and a key element in assuring the presence of a "safe" homosexual population), late hours of operation (midnight to 8:00 a.m.), and in some cases, such as the Zoo and the Barn, a combination of stand-up bar features with a dance floor.

All of the settings were unmarked, and carefully located in a deserted area of the West Village.[12] They were carefully kept unpretentious. The Zoo, for example, located in a block-long row of meat-packing houses, could not be distinguished in any way from the other buildings surrounding it. The outside facade appeared like any other meat-packing building. A single door, painted a dull red and somewhat abused looking, was marked with only the street number. A peephole burrowed through the door which was bolted shut at all times. To enter, a bell was rung. The peephole would jolt open and a pair of inquiring eyes inspected those seeking entrance. Membership cards passed through the peephole and the door opened. An entrance fee was charged once inside. At the Zoo, a second locked door followed the first. Entrance money was collected between them.

The immediate and lasting popularity of the pig parlors devolved on two elements: they reinforced homosexual identity statements and the expressive gratification accruing in making these statements, and they facilitated direct sexual activity in a highly secret, illegal atmosphere with similar, desirable identities. Whereas the regular gay bar reinforces identity, the prohibition on open sexual contact casts a mundane pall over participation. The gay bath, described below, severely reduces the expressive elements in creating an erotic identity, complicating sexual communications. Although encouraging open sexual intercourse, the baths have become an everyday part of the urban landscape, again generating a taken-for-grantedness that reduces the sexual tension associated with illicit endeavors. The pig parlor, always subject to police raids, was the most exciting combination of both worlds.

It was a world of silence, devoted to serious erotic posturing (in full gear) and sexual contact. Communications took place via body idiom and the eyes. Within this mass of movement individuals slipped in and out of the orgy room. Some individuals positioned themselves outside the door waiting to follow the entrance of a desired object of interest. Others stationed themselves on the opposite, dark side of the door that also permitted visual view of new entrants. New-found lovers trailed each other through the doorway, hand in hand to prevent separation in the darkness. The unwanted, or merely hungry, entered the dark room as soon as they entered the bar. Remaining inside for the entire evening, they gorged on as much sex as possible.

In contrast to the color, noise, and movement of the bar outside, the orgy room was small, dark, static, crowded, oppressively hot, and deadly silent. The throb of the outside bar seemed to be smothered by the deep absorption of the individual concentrating on finding his way about the darkened room. With the exception of the sucking sounds of fellatio, or the wet gasping sound of a penis pulled out of an anus, there was total silence.

Painstakingly created images, so carefully prepared for the visual phases of the bar, were promptly set aside in the orgy room, and replaced by the phantoms of erotic fantasy brought to life by the mass of touching bodies in the encircling darkness. Interaction took place between physical entities (if liaisons were not prearranged in other parts of the bar).[13] Only the glory hole setting offers a similar eclipse of visual identity, but even there the penis can be seen.[14] The nature of erotic activity within the orgy room precluded knowing those with whom one engaged in sex. Don E passed his penis from mouth to mouth without knowing who they belonged to. Tony C plunged into the "suck room," got blown, withdrew, resumed dancing, and plunged in again for more.

NOTES

1. "Piss-elegance" refers to a style of presentation that is seen as "pseudo" authentic and thus false. The style emphasizes conservative attire and formal manners. The image is closely associated with the "closeted" homosexual and middle class virtues. The style is also associated with pecuniary success, which many participants have not attained. "Elegance" — meaning monied manners — is pretended and hence labeled "piss." Patrons of these bars do not refer to themselves as "piss-elegant" although they employ the term when referring to others whom they wish to derogate.

2. It was during one of the first of many observations at the Stud that Dr. E pointed out the crucial role of the jukebox for a bar's success, and the type of population it attracts. The Stud's jukebox played the most contemporary, popular music. It blasted away unceasingly. The crowd tended to be young through middle age. The Triangle's jukebox was western, featuring country music. Its population tended to be western to leather, and late 30s and up. The Piano Bar has an outdated jukebox. The population, always meager, tends to be late middle age, unsophisticated in attire, and best described as colorless.

3. Cues to erotic identity and roles are very complex. During 1974 and 1975, hankies became one major source of cueing others into sexual identities and roles. A retail store in Cherry Grove issued a small but extensive pocket-sized chart of the sexual meanings of colors and positions of hankies. See "Crossing Signals", *Time,* 1975.

4. This individual once wore a teeshirt designed with a large "9" on the chest. Henceforth, the observer designated him "Number 9." Number 9 has been observed many times in various settings. He frequents western to leather bars, a particular gay bath, and summers at The Pines on Fire Island.

5. The tip of the thumb and forefinger grasp the cigarette, while the other fingers and portion of hand form a cup around the cigarette. The cigarette is never held between the tips of the forefinger and middle finger. This grasp is associated with the flamboyant set and piss-elegant queen. From the perspective of the patron of The Stud, or any like typed bar, the latter marks a "nelly" or effeminate individual.

6. There are exceptions to this general practice. M a bald-headed man, slimly but tightly built, had amazingly penetrating eyes. Alert, wide open, always clear, and shining brilliantly, his eyes pierced the armor of the best maintained imagery. Invariably, M entered a bar, glanced fiercely about, seized upon the object of his choice, sent him a devastating stare, and without fail, succeeded in his endeavors. His apparent attitude was surly (hence masculine); and the magnetism of the eyes, the good build, and finely chiseled face, made him a "star" on any bar's horizon (he never exhibited his genitals).

7. See Sasha R. Weitman (1973: 217–238) for an illuminating discussion on "affection" in private versus public settings with reference to the simultaneous concerns of including some while excluding others during erotic dialogues.

8. Various bar populations react differently to individual conduct. The Eagle, for example, is mainly used for posturing. Hours pass by in which participants pose in a favorite posture in their "spot." Little communication seems to be passing between patrons. The great detail devoted to posturing indicates that it is an expressive gratification in itself. The individual is expected to remain aloof for hours on end. However, anyone concentrating on the same type of in-depth posturing in friendlier bars, where mixing is stressed, would be

reacted to as conceited or affected. The crowd at the Nichol Bar would be offended if the individual entered and isolated himself by heavy posturing.

9. Verbally concluding an unreciprocated visual dialogue directed at the observer one patron, after feeling the observer's arms and indicating a desire to be "fist-fucked" (a sexual activity in which the hand/wrist are inserted into the anus and followed by a pumping action), whispered into the observer's ear that he hoped the observer was not like the trick with whom he went home the previous night. Dressed from head to foot in leather, this patron thought he had himself a "butch." Arriving at the trick's pad he discovered silk sheets on the bed. He got so enraged that he almost vomited. Cutting the narrator short, the observer excused himself to purchase a new beer, and relocated. By the way, the whole story could have been fabricated. Relating such narratives is one technique by which the authenticity of an individual's identity can be directly tested. Responses to the story are weighed and analyzed before the pursuit is pressed forward.

10. According to many informants involved in the city's gay life for several decades, the years between 1954 and 1966 were exceptionally oppressive for gay people. Vice squad activity consistently occurred in all known homosexual oases. Undercover agents infiltrated bars, baths, public toilets, and parks. After the new mayor took office, the atmosphere changed. "Tom Burke has written ("The New Homosexuality," *Esquire,* December, 1969), that John Lindsay had barely been sworn in before Dick Leitsch, the Mattachine's vociferous director, rose at one of the Mayor's town meetings to denounce entrapment of homosexuals by police. Even as he spoke, a plainclothesman was entraping an innocent but effete young man in the back room of Julius Bar, Greenwich Village. An Episcopal minister (who had stopped in the bar for a sandwich) witnessed this, and phoned another minister, who phoned the Mayor and almost everyone else of any importance with a listed number. The result was a meeting in a village cafe attended by an influential heterosexual group that included the Mayor, the police commissioner, the police commissioner's wife, Allen Ginsberg, the Civil Liberties Union and The Fugs. Entrapment ended the next morning." From Don Teal, 1971: 26.

11. Pornographic movies were being shown in some bars to encourage business before the Zoo opened. The Spike was one of them. This began a trend toward more blatant sexuality in bars that rapidly culminated in the pig parlor.

12. The past tense is used in these paragraphs because all of the original pig parlors were closed in one gigantic raid that took place in the early morning hours on July 19, 1971 (see *The New York Times,* July 19, 1971). However, in February, 1975, the "A" bar opened hosting similar activities. Additional bar openings quickly followed. A new generation of pig parlors continues to exist as of this writing.

13. Physical identities are not "merely" physical objects. Bodies are

associated with erotic identities, mental images complementing scarce, if not altogether absent, perceivable qualities of the individual. See the above discussion of "ideal types."

14. The "meat rack" between the Fire Island communities of Cherry Grove and The Pines occasionally becomes as dark as the orgy room during some nights. Tree enshrouded, a cloudy, misty, moonless evening creates a black landscape. The white markings painted on tree trunks as guides to walking among the bushes disappear. Individuals bump into trees and each other, and occasionally fall into depressions of swamp. On such nights, identity and interaction are much like the orgy room of the pig parlor. The faintest moon, however, brightens the sandy paths restoring vision as the medium for sexual negotiations.

chapter 7

The Gay Bath
A Perpetual World of Sex

THE STRIPPING OF IDENTITY

Unlike any other setting previously discussed, the homosexual bath is devoted exclusively to immediate sexual gratification. To further this cause, the bath stage is set up so that the patron's attention is never allowed to stray from the focus of explicit sexuality.

Impersonality and anonymity are carried to an extreme. Upon entrance, all identity pegs, including clothing and jewelry (with a few exceptions described below), are replaced by a singular towel. The uniformity in staging areas standardizes any idiosyncratic claims of individuals: Rooms and lockers are minimally furnished. No unique feature exists by which an individual can mold some personal, extraordinary claim about himself. Claims to interest narrowly devolve on the physicality of the individual, creative

use of the towel, attitude, and self-presentation brought out in physical grooming, style of walk, and mannerisms. This anonymity frees the individual from inhibitions that prevail in less controlled, less safe, more ambivalent settings. Communications preceding liaisons are briefer and more to the point. Physical contact occurs without much ritualistic foreplay although successful transactions usually involve a brief period of courting and mutual exchanges of consent. Rejection, always possible, is not felt as keenly as in other public settings. The high degree of anonymity helps assuage its pain, and the abundance of erotic opportunities reduces its significance. Depending on where it occurs — in the private room, orgy room, or hall — rejection, still discomforting, can be accepted without loss of face and thus promotes a more aggressive attitude toward sexual conquests. A very tall, light-skinned black, in his mid-30s and looking sluggish in appearance, for example, was observed several evenings at the "E" Bath. Walking down the halls or into rooms he would unceremoniously approach an individual, smile, and immediately reach for the patron's groin. Invariably, his hand was pushed aside or a muffled "no thank you" was heard. Undaunted and still smiling, he would turn away and repeat the same approach with the nearest individual.

Total anonymity does not result in a normless mass of erotic pleasure. Forms of sociation guide behavior as in other erotic settings. Certain areas of the bath are utilized for some interaction but not others. Nudity is permitted, but not everywhere. If rejection is to be kept to a bare minimum, expected forms of behavior are adhered to. The reader is also reminded that every patron carries within his head an ideal of the perfect sex object and the most exciting sexual "scene." No one can discern these ideals without clues. An audacious overture concludes in failure. To avoid rejection, communications precede overtures unless strong signals of enticement or approval discourage the need to do so. Thus the bath, like the gay bar, public toilet, and spontaneous encounter, is a vast network of complex silent communications. While posturing his "hardware," the individual simultaneously reads the reactions of others toward his portrayal, fends off unwanted advances, and encourages interesting and promising overtures.

THE PHYSICAL PLANT

The exterior facade of the gay bath mirrors conventional surroundings. It complements the containing neighborhood. A curtain of inconspicuousness diminishes interest in the establishment and unobtrusively integrates it into the urban landscape. The Continental, housed in a handsome building recently proclaimed a historical landmark, for example, is located in a middle income neighborhood of apartment buildings. The entrance is tucked into a far corner of the building, away from major flows of "conventional" traffic. It opens directly onto the street. Only the grey painted windows differentiate the three bath floors from all the others. The "E," the oldest bath in the city, is located in a light manufacturing area of the city. Although occupying an architecturally interesting building, the busy business world of day and the surrounding emptiness of night seem to miss the boldly announced "BATHS" cemented into the sidewalk.

Never has the observer noticed a line of admission in front of a bath establishment that would evoke unwanted attention. Entrance areas are large enough to absorb the sporadic arrival of several patrons. Random departures generate little if any interest. The clientele does not dress eccentrically. During the business day, patrons show up in business attire, perfectly normal and not noteworthy. Evening patrons arrive in acceptable leisure clothing. Even when the "M" Country generated heavy business by dropping Tuesday rates to $1.00 per person, attracting mammoth numbers at one time, the large foyer swallowed up the crowds.

The baths share a common physical structure that only varies in detail given plant size and layout. A choice of three types of accommodation is offered to the customer — the private room, either single or double, the walk-in locker, and the gym locker. Prices of an accommodation are based on the amount of room and privacy each offers. The number of hours the price purchases per accommodation fluctuates within the week. Prices are more expensive on weekends, buying less time at some establishments (the "E," for example, leases space for eight-hour intervals on weekends but for 12-hour intervals Monday through Thursday).

Rooms are the most expensive rental and highly popular. A bed, a single low-watt bulb, a couple of hangers for clothing, and an ashtray furnish the tiny cubicles. Popular because they offer the choice between private or public sex, the room can also be used for staging sexual identities that other accommodations cannot.

Walk-in lockers are narrow closets equipped with a singular bench, hangers for attire, and one low-watt bulb. They offer privacy for sexual encounters (in vertical positions), and can be used for some posturing. Both walk-in and room rentals hint at "background" identities by virtue of the visible clothing hanging therein.

The cheapest rental, the gym locker, is a small cubicle that houses only clothing and other personal belongings. Each bath has a "dormitory" for the walk-in or gym locker patron who wants to rest during his stay at the baths. Dormitory beds are accessible to all. Rest, however, is inevitably disturbed by those seeking erotic activity, particularly by the corps of old and misshapen men who cannot make out elsewhere.

Baths include snack bars, rest areas, and television rooms, permitting lengthy periods of attendance. The price of admission offers economic rationale for prolonging attendance as long as possible. Erotic horizons are never confined to a single or dual sexual encounter but to a series of sexual encounters with one or more sexual partners. Even as patrons rest, they remain involved in the never-ending erotic activities. Watching the passing parade of cruising patrons and hearing the sounds of erotic activity, attendance is an entirely engrossing affair. One informant claimed 17 sexual encounters during a 12-hour visitation, while another disclosed he "did" over 20.

TIMELESSNESS

No matter the time of day or evening, the type of surrounding neighborhood and exterior happenings of the conventional world, the interior atmosphere of the bath is held constant. The only signals of change are new arrivals, variously attired — perhaps indicating the passage of time (e.g., from work to leisure attire and vice versa, indicating a change in the major routines of the everyday world) — their number varying with the time of day, and the few clocks on interior walls that visually, but silently, signify the passage of time. Painted or shuttered windows not only closet sexual activities from inquiring eyes on the outside, but prevent the attention of patrons from wandering to the outside world. No sun or moon accompanies this carefully constructed timelessness — there is only the amount of time purchased at the door. Dim orange light maintains an even intensity in the long hallways 24 hours a day. No unusual noise intrudes on the carefully shielded scene, unless connected with unfolding interior activities. The rhythmic tingle of keys, dangling from the wrist or calf of the patron, orchestrate the steady, perpetual flow of the sexual quest. Loud slaps, deep groans, or even yells, punctuate the endless, whispered motion, as an encounter explodes into a sadomasochistic romp, or concludes in the ecstacies of orgasm. From entrance to departure, consciousness is coaxed into and maintained within these timeless erotic parameters.

PERSONAL PREPARATIONS
AND SEXUAL IMAGERY

Having been furnished with only a towel and a small, expandable bracelet holding the key to this accommodation and a round metal tag impressed with the number thereof, the patron enters the fantastical realm of perpetual sex.

The only item of attire worn at the baths is the towel. Indeed, baths prohibit wearing attire except for certain sexual accouterments. Towels are folded in various styles, making statements as to the sexual aspirations of the wearer, and emphasizing parts of the body the individual wishes to stress. One man in his early 40s, for example, arranges the towel in such a way that the gathering point opens at the groin, revealing a large and fat penis.

If the individual wishes to be really blatant, he casually walks about the setting, towel in hand. The stride notice-ably bounces the penis and testes with each step. If the buttocks are to be shown in an attempt to attract anal interaction, the towel is draped around the body so that the cloth comes together above the cheeks of the buttocks. These are the most obvious towel techniques used to attract individuals with specific sexual goals in mind.

Towel styles are not only used for indicating specific sexual roles but also for enhancing somatic features. Some patrons do not fold the towel, allowing it to fall full length. If they have trim bodies, the top of the towel hangs casually above the base of the penis, pubic hairs exposed. This style highlights the slimness of the waist and upper torso. The average bathgoer, however, simply folds the towel in half and wraps it around his middle.

A few patrons bring towels from home. The texture, color, or size of the towel is thought to enhance some physical feature of the wearer. One black-haired individual wore a dark green towel that effectively emphasized the color of his hair, eyes, and skin complexion.

A second reason for bringing one's own towel is to prevent the illicit replacement of a dry towel for a wet one when hung up before entering the steamroom or shower. Having taken many showers, or soaked for long periods of time in the steamroom or sauna, patrons will have soiled their towel. They will not hesitate replacing it with a dry one, if available at the shower rack. Wetness of the towel by the way has significance for bath communication. Those wearing wet towels are assumed to have been at the bath for some time. As a corollary, the patron is thought to have already engaged in many sexual adventures and is seen as no longer sexually acute. A new arrival on the other hand is fresh and wearing a dry towel. As one technique of information control, a spare towel accompanies the well-prepared individual.

If the towel is the most widely worn item at the bath, it is not the only one. Tim, for example, wears a jockstrap when cruising the halls carrying the towel in one hand. Penis and testes bulge prominently outward in the support. Due to the structure of the jockstrap, the entire buttocks is visible (and touchable). Each buttock cheek flexes as he walks, drawing much attention from surrounding others.

Idiosyncratic towels, jockstraps, leather equipage, and several other kinds of accouterment indicate that a bath visit is not a spontaneous decision. Only the after-business-hour crowd arriving directly from work could be described as a spontaneous one. They arrive in nothing more than business attire. However, many individuals plan a night at the baths, and arrive with an attache case brimming with appropriate bath accessories. Preparations not only include personal towels, but cans of grease to be used in "fist-fucking"; large, rubber dildos for exotic anal penetration; belts for sado-masochistic scenes; and conventional "K-Y" (a neutral lubricant) for "regular" anal sodomy. These accessories are prominently displayed to advertise particular forms of sexual virtuosity. One individual observed at "E" Bath laces black leather straps around the upper thighs, penis, and testes. On one side hangs a large ring of keys. Deodorant, personal soap, and mouthwash also accompany the patron and have the same effect of maintaining "freshness" as wearing a dry towel described above.

Some preparations extend far beyond the above. Gil, for example, takes drugs before going to the baths. He uses windowpane, mescaline, blotter, or sunshine. Drugs increase the number of orgasms he can attain. Because he is into the anal scene, i.e., penetrating someone's anus with his penis or vice versa, and because these drugs tend to cause diarrhea, he fasts the entire day preceding bath attendance. Just before leaving for the baths, he takes an enema to make sure the colon is clean.

Alex, on the other hand, does not fast before going to the bath. He takes repeated enemas until the lower bowel tract is clean. During sex, Alex likes to switch between oral and anal sodomy without stopping to clean off, thus requiring the absence of any contaminating fecal matter. Tony C. pointed out to the observer that anyone into the anal scene, whether rimming, anal intercourse, or fist-fucking, has to have taken adequate preparations to be clean. The first sign of fecal matter suspends all interaction.

Fecal matter is not always a "turn-off" in erotic activity. The following blurb was taken from a wall in one of the toilet stalls at the "E" Bath: "Slave needs master, especially dig shit, piss, cock-ball-tit torture, humiliation, dog-training, etc. Will wait in room 202, SIR." The walls of "E's" three toilets are covered with hundreds of advertisements concerning "piss and shit" transactions.

Exotic equipment is usually confined to rooms, with a few exceptions noted in walk-in lockers. Giant dildos and one-pound cans of grease are not hauled around bath premises. Not only cumbersome, they do not fit into the normative expectations of bath functioning.

EROTIC NEGOTIATIONS

There is remarkable restraint between patrons given the blatant sexual atmosphere of the bath. The fear of rejection creates some restraint, although it is not strongly feared in many areas of the bath. It is the search for an erotic ideal that contributes to restraint. The quest for the "right" partner and the most exciting "scene" inhibit impatience.

Hallways, like streets, are conduits between bath areas and the major arteries for cruising. The new arrival inevitably hits the hallways to survey as much of the population as possible before settling down to any one area for making out. Continuously busy peering into poorly lit rooms, walk-in closets, and at opposite flowing traffic, the endless stream of patrons walk down the narrow passageways, keys tingling with the swing of their gait. Back and forth in halls and up and down between floors, patrons fashion a perpetual party of sexual explorers. Only intermittent showers, brief rest periods, and occasional use of sauna and steamroom interrupt the flow of movement.

Eye contact usually begins a dialogue. As in other erotic settings, a penetrating look shot into another patron's eyes is a significant indication of interest. Because the entire population present in the hallways is interested in responding to erotic signals and can do so rather directly, visual advances must be carefully controlled to prevent unwanted overtures. An accidental glance may result in an undesired physical advance. Therefore, the individual quickly sweeps those approaching him in the hallway, reserving significant glances for only those in whom he is interested. He studiously looks away from anyone he wishes to avoid. In such cases, eyes stare directly ahead or peer into rooms to evade any mistaken visual contact.

Fondling the chest, neck, arms, and groin follows reciprocal eye contact. Kisses may be exchanged in the gradual absorption of increasing involvement. Developing erections deepen the advance. Finally, the couple head for the accommodation of one or the other, the public dormitory, or orgy room.

As soon as two (or more) patrons get together in a public area, others quickly flock around the scene, either to vicariously participate in or actually join the encounter. For example, two muscular individuals discovered each other in the hallway, mutually signified interest, and joined each other. As they embraced an older man began touching one of the pair's buttocks. His hand was rudely shoved aside. Those watching were warned that no interference would be tolerated. However, the gaping crowd did not disperse, but anxiously waited for the pair to have sex. The pair finally disappeared into a walk-in locker that literally shook with activity. (The occupant of the adjacent walk-in locker yelled over, "Hey, you're knocking down the goddam wall!")

Visually perceivable physical features of the body sometimes indicate a patron's erotic roles and sexual practices. For example, heavy nipple work — pinching, biting, sucking, and clamping — tend to develop distended nipples. As an example, Richard C., a professional actor, has rather large nipples for this reason. During sex, he continually instructs sex partners to "squeeze harder" or "bite those tits, baby." One bearded man in his mid-thirties has pierced ears, tits, and foreskin. Having placed small hoops through the nipples, he asks partners to pull on them. Distended nipples are visually noticeable and indicate to any would-be partner that the patron expects some concentration, perhaps heavy, on his nipples during erotic episodes, and probably will expect to administer the same on his partner. Steve B. explains to the observer that he cannot "come" (have an orgasm) if his "tits" are not heavily sucked and fondled during sex. Not everyone enjoys this activity and will shun those who seem to expect it. On the other hand, those who desire it associate certain physical types with doing it. The guy has to be a muscle-builder, and ready to dominate the sexual encounter for Steve B. He would not dream of permitting a "nelly" to suck his nipples.

Tactile cues also indicate sexual preferences and roles. Those who fondle the buttocks frequently during the initial stages of an encounter evince a strong wish for anal intercourse. Those who continually return to the anal region during the meeting demonstrate a preference for it.

Hallways are avenues of display, conduits of communication, and passageways of courtship. It is not uncommon to see couples and groups of individuals in various stages of love-making. But if hands occassionally grasp a penis in the hallway, never once has a full-blown sexual episode been observed there.

Practical considerations inhibit open eroticism in the halls. The large number of people in the corridors, particularly the legion of undesirables who "always try to horn in," encourage activity relocation to a room or walk-in locker. Many men do not like to be observed when engaging in sex, while others demand it as part of their sexual fantasy.

The former prefer the privacy of rooms or lockers. Furthermore, those who relish anal penetration, fist-fucking, or other esoteric forms of sexual transactions require accessories not convenient for hallway work, e.g., a prone position requiring a bed, grease, and perhaps a large dildo for dilating the anus before the fist is inserted.

"ALLEGORICAL" MESSAGES

As small, individual "sets" rooms are enlisted to champion postured identities. The standardized and barren appointment of the room directs all attention to the occupant. Because clothes are visibly hung in the room, they can be employed as indices to the occupant's erotic identity. Special cruising clothes are worn to foster specific impressions. Leather jacket, jeans, plaid shirt, wide belt, and large boots cast an aura of masculinity around the nude individual reclining on the bed.

Some rooms remain dark, the occupants daring others to come in and investigate. Extensively used by undesirables, particularly the obese and aged, few individuals are temerous enough to accept the invitation. The end result is hours of neglect for those who lie there.

Those who hope to entice preferred sexual types into the room, but who do not effect rigid sexual postures, lie on their backs, the head propped against the pillow, which rests against the wall opposite the doorway. The towel usually covers the genital area, but not always. One middle-aged white male with a large penis lies on the bed, as described above, with legs spread open so that the penis hangs down onto the mattress or across one thigh. He occasionally strokes it to maintain a semi-erection (never full, so that there is promise of even greater expansion). Those who wear towels continually massage the penis to keep it erect, causing a protrusion in the towel, exciting interest because of the mystery surrounding the hidden penis causing the bulge. Others simply neglect the genitals until someone comes into the room. A leg may be raised to cast shadow around the groin area, heightening the mystery of what "he's got." Eyes face the door and for good reason. The individual is not only interested in attracting the right sexual object, requiring perception of and visual communication with the individual to do so, but is also concerned with controlling those who enter the room. He refuses entrance to undesirables as he welcomes "Mr. Right."

Some patrons differentiate little between others attracted to the erotic roles they proffer. Within the past three years (1973-1975) for example, the "E" Bath has attracted an increasing number of individuals who enjoy highly esoteric sexual practices. Placing personal advertisements on toilet walls, they announce what type of sex they want (see above) and with whom. One advertisement concludes, "if door is shut, knock twice," indicating that it does not matter who responds to the graffiti. The respondent merely shows up and follows through with the advertised action. If the patron grows weary in waiting for results of the advertisement, he stages a presentation in the room. A middle-aged male, for instance, reclines on his back in the room, having placed an enormous rubber dildo between spread legs. A sizable container of grease rests near his side. (A can of grease on the bed without a dildo signifies a desire to be fist-fucked). This individual obviously wants to be penetrated by the dildo and possibly a fist. He sometimes poses with two or three fingers tucked into his anus, longingly looking at the passing traffickers. Sexual practice rather than physical or presentational qualities of the individual matter in the selection of an erotic mate for these individuals.

Another prevalently postured identity is the individual who wants anal intercourse. He lies on the bed on his stomach, the anus facing the door. The towel is set aside. Sometimes the pillow is tucked underneath the groin area, propping the buttocks up. The individual does not care who enters the room and penetrates him. He often neglects turning around to look. A youthful, prematurely grey-haired man spends all evening in such a position. At least ten men were noted to have had intercourse with him during one evening (the door never closed).

Sado-masochistic posturing also takes place. One heavy-set man, lying face down on his bed, places a thick belt across the buttocks, signaling a wish to be flagellated by those who notice.

Other erotic roles include the "cocksucker." One individual lies at an end of his bed near the door on his back, with legs braced upright against the wall. His head dangles over the edge of the bed, the tongue suggestively moving back and forth in a licking fashion. Another cocksucker pose is squatting on the haunches on the floor near the the door, head at crotch level. Anyone passing by is waved at and encouraged to enter.

Posturing is a creative undertaking and impossible to completely describe. As pointed out in the above, gesturing dichotomizes into two general categories: that which demands mutual communication and that which makes a simple statement about sexual expectations. Anyone attracted by the latter simply enters the room and follows through. Protracted negotations are unnecessary.

Signs of approval between hallway traffickers and room occupants do not assure sexual success. After the onlooker enters the room, touches are exchanged. These are crucial signals into the erotic intentions of the individual. During initial touching, either patron may find the body or sexual expectations of the other individual incompatible with his. "No, thank you" concludes the overture. If the entrant finds the room occupant uninteresting after touching him, he simply drifts out of the room and continues his travels. If both are pleased with the other, the door closes and sex commences. In some cases the door remains ajar, an open invitation for others to come in and join the encounter.

Some individuals simply walk from room to room, whether or not the occupant approves. In such cases the room occupant employs various techniques for getting rid of the unwanted visitor. The simplest and most courteous rejection is a quietly spoken "No, thank you." Other occupants merely lie silent, not reacting at all (certainly not developing an erection if the penis is touched) as the intruder rummages over the body. Evoking no reaction, the intruder gets bored and departs. Other favorite spoken comments at such times are, "I'm just resting," or "I've just come." The final resolution to an obdurate intruder is shoving him out the door, barring his entrance with a leg, or pushing his hand aside in a rude manner.

Sexual encounters usually culminate with someone's orgasm. Orgasm in the baths, unlike the tearoom, does not terminate erotic participation. The bath is a carefully controlled arena encouraging innumerable sexual encounters. The individual who has had an orgasm withdraws and moves onto rest or new envelopments, while those with whom he was involved either continue the encounter with someone else, rest, or search for new partners. The steady, persistent sexual motif never abates. One's identity as a sexual object is not threatened by orgasm. After some time for rest, or no time at all, the individual is ready to reassert a sexual identity. Continuous sex is enhanced by the fact that the baths attract new arrivals throughout the day and night, providing fresh faces and identities.

Inevitably, a point is reached beyond which patrons lose interest in continuing the sexual quest. Satiation, the lateness of the hour, the nature of the crowd, various causes of frustration (a series of bad sexual experiences), or the exhaustion of time purchased at the bath, prompt the patron to terminate participation.

chapter 8
Public Settings, Identities, Roles and Erotic Interaction
The Universality of Silent Discourse

ACCOUNTS OF NATIONAL AND INTERNATIONAL SETTINGS

The foregoing has covered a diverse number of public settings utilized by the silent community for staging erotic identities and engaging in erotic dialogues. In spite of the variation in the facultive quality of the setting, ranging from the highly ambiguous street encounter to the tightly structured setting of the leather bar, e.g., The Eagle, community relations are characterized by silence, gestural means of communication, cautious statements of intention, impersonality, and anonymity. Using the body as the center of communication, virtual identity is conjectured and imputed on the bases of where the transaction takes place, the time, and the various staging devices that create

and assuage doubt. Without verbal discourse to complicate communication, without conventional acceptance that would legitimate illicit intentions requiring a different form of sociation, and as long as homosexual, erotic action takes place in public, is it not safe to assume that the variables of silent community work, e.g., publicness, silence, impersonality, anonymity, and eroticism will facilitate encounters in similar settings on a national and international basis?

The question leads to the last frontier of public erotic work, but one that cannot be entirely substantiated by firsthand data.[1] Because the observer's study was confined mostly to the environs of New York City, the information concerning national and international settings is largely anecdotal.

That there is a national and international silent community, however, cannot be doubted. Silence prevents linquistic barriers to communication on an international level; eroticism provides a common topic of interaction between shared, understandable identities and roles; ubiquitous and similar public settings contour forms of social mediation that emphasize quiet, gestural, covert cueing while carefully avoiding dramatic, stigma-evoking ones; and impersonality and anonymity recommend participation in spite of national and international culture differences.

It has been shown that silent community work cuts across class and ethnic lines in the United States and Canada. The park in Brooklyn includes white, middle to upper income men, black youths from a low income project, and middle income black men from a nearby, racially mixed, cooperative housing development.

The extensive observations of toilets located in institutions and subways illustrate the wide appeal silent community work enjoys, and the diversity of participants it attracts. Based on data from the urban area, it would seem that the silent community should be a viable one on the national and international level. Is it?

First, Dr. E moved to two large, northeastern cities during the course of the study. He invited the observer for a tour of each. The tours included such sites as gay bars, public parks, and toilets, a "dirty" book store, and the baths. Communications and participation in each flowed as described above.

Second, the observer completed a narrow motor tour of the midwest and northeast of the United States and Canada. In St. Louis, Peoria, Chicago, Toronto, Montreal, Quebec City, and communities of the northeast (Bangor, Boston, and Provincetown), the silent community proved fully functional and accessible. In Quebec City, where French is emphasized, one merely walks on the esplanade near a landmark hotel, or strolls through the grounds of a historic fort, and contact with the silent community is assured. Language proves no barrier.

Third, a trip to Atlanta, Georgia, and a public erotic tour provided by John R revealed similar facts. John R's rural experiences in the south have been noted above.

Again, leather weekend at Cherry Grove, Fire Island, during the early summer of 1975 hosted at least 300 German participants flown over for the occasion. Language and communication could have been a problem but leather attire, self-presentations, and "typified" identities resolved most communication and interactional barriers.

Carlo and Joe traveled to Italy, Greece, Spain, Portugal, Egypt, and Morocco. Without reference to "gay" guides to Europe and Africa, they cruised public parks at night with considerable success. They indicated that park cruising was much the same as that of the United States. They also ran into a friend in Athens who worked public tearooms. Aside from complaining that the Greeks were beautiful people but "inordinately small" (referring to the size of the penis), tearoom work was much like that at home. Carlo and Joe tried it and agree.

Stanley F relates that he took a European tour in 1965. Except for an anonymously published mimeographed list of notoriously inaccurate gay addresses, no references existed to gay locations. In stopovers in Edinburgh and Glasglow, Stanley failed to establish any homosexual contacts. Continual rain prevented park adventures and the reference list proved totally inaccurate. In London, he managed to find a private club on a very narrow street just off Trafalgar Square. Club patrons furnished Stanley an accurate list of gay hotels and private clubs in Amsterdam, his next stop. After spending a "wild" week of sexual pleasure in Amsterdam, he journeyed to Copenhagen, utilizing resources gathered in Holland. From Copenhagen, he traveled to Cologne, Germany, but was unable to find any of the gay bars furnished by friends in Copenhagen. He walked about Cologne and stumbled on a public, subterranean toilet located near a pedestrian shopping mall. It was a very active tearoom. He met one man from Augsburg who took him to another outside toilet situated along the then-flooding Rhine. The next evening another contact from the same toilet led Stanley to an empty lot. Stanley then traveled to Nurenburg and Munich. He found the famed Zanzibar Bar, a piss-elegant gay bar in Munich. He cruised there most of the time. He also cruised the many public parks with equal degrees of success. In recounting his experiences, the processes of cruising were similar to those employed in domestic settings.

Bob D informed the observer that when he was stationed in Germany with the United States Army, he used public toilets for cruising that were located in a vast park that formed a large, green horseshoe around a beautiful baroque palace. He cruised mostly at dusk or early evening. Maneuvering was much like that of domestic tearoom scenes. German toilets, he recalled, unlike American facilities, have long troughs as urinals instead of individual units. Visibility is facilitated by this arrangement because there are no sides on individual units behind which the genitals can be hidden. Bob states that he entered the small park structures and often found at least five or six individuals nestled around the trough. With his arrival, erect penes were held down until his identity could be established. Bob would squeeze into the line along the trough, remain standing a few seconds without urinating, and then begin cautious auto-manipulation. Not long thereafter, the Germans would make similar overtures and an encounter would unfold. Bob also related that the toilets in the Bahnhofs (train stations) of the many

German cities he visited were also used for erotic activities.

Because all of the above accounts involved American men and foreign nationals, the observer was curious as to whether foreign nationals cruising other foreign nationals operated along silent community lines. In conversing with H. K., an emigre from West Germany who arrived in New York City approximately five years ago, the observer learned that not only do Germans "love" outdoor work (public tearoom and park settings), public cruising in Germany is very much like that in the United States. His description of cruising techniques and their spatial and temporal placement were very similar to those described by others to the observer about settings abroad, and directly observed by him in the United States. H. K. had no problem, in fact, establishing erotic contacts in France where he briefly studied, or in Brussels, Belgium, where he worked for two years. Interviews with Helmuth S., Felix, and W confirm H. K.'s experiences and description of them.

To make a tentative judgment, it seems that the social and ecological circumstances of the silent community indeed contribute to a very viable and adaptive form of participation over time on a national and international level.

NOTE

1. Several gay guides have been published that list the full range of meeting places in both the United States and abroad. For example, see John Frances Hunter's *The Gay Insider*, 1971, and his *Gay Insider, USA*, 1972.

chapter 9

"The Closet," Strangers, "Scenes," and Moral Order

MOTIVATING SOCIOLOGICAL FACTORS

Homosexuals view the conventional world as a "heterosexually" defined reality. It is not only threatening in the sense that the homosexual has to hide the knowledge of secret sexual interests to evade social stigma (whether real or imagined) and to be able to live an "uncomplicated" life; and artificial in the sense that he has to actively and consciously sustain the constellation of normative expectations and roles of "male" (without reference to homosexual values) that are expected in other-than homosexual situations.[1] The homosexual does not "feel" the same about conventional society as heterosexual males do who he assumes to be "spontaneously" tied into the moral order of

155

society by an internalized, taken-for-granted masculinity. The homosexual has a different set of erotic relevances and interests, which cannot be "wished away" but must be hidden (so he feels) for fear of identity disclosure. He feels constrained to embrace and manage, in varying degrees of biographic depth, an identity consistent with a hetero-sexually defined, socially presumed, self-definition of "male" when participating in conventional situations, while deny-ing by concealment and failure of disclosure, the identity he considers authentic that is based on the psycho-biological reality of his sexual orientation. The intensive management of self as homosexual in a heterosexual society points to two sociological factors that motivate the individual to conceal his identity and seek frequent if tenuous homo-sexual ties through public eroticism.

The first factor is the avoidance of social stigma. To avoid stigma commonsense reality is drastically altered into something that demands intensive attention to self-manage-ment and information control (see Gofmman, 1959).

The second fator, a socio-psychological one, has reper-cussions for the self-conception of the homosexual indi-vidual and the irrelevance that heterosexual situations have for him as a "male." This factor is the lack of masculinity ("I, a homosexual, cannot be a man") that commonsense notions would have us believe of him through its effemi-nate/pervert stereotype of the homosexual.

These two factors strongly encourage a dichotomy in the social reality of the homosexual that is routinized and stabilized into two distinct spheres of activity. The hetero-sexual sphere, whenever it consciously emerges in the mind of the homosexual, requires a subjectively felt artifi-cial role play at "male" with appropriate behavior, interests, and presentations. And the homosexual sphere where so-called heterosexual "pretenses" can be dropped and homo-sexual identities and activities played out.

Erotic situations legitimate the identity of the homo-sexual, but this is the point: the homosexual's erotic orienta-tion is the major criterion of inclusion in subcultural situa-tions. Sexuality is the differentiating criterion of belonging. The individual is expected to share and expects sexual others to share the interests, activities, expectations, and identity portrayals that are part of these sexual situations. Eroticism, with its implications for identity and sociability, is the ever-present relevance in such settings. But what sexuality? As homosexual males, they share general erotic expectations and interests, but they have idiosyncratic biographies, which include divergent sexual interests and experiences, different images of themselves and others, and dissimilar sexual expectations. They may or may not share identical, compatible, and complementary erotic notions with another individual. As biological males, there is neither a "natural" division of labor in erotic transactions nor commonly accepted definitions of what makes for compatible sex roles. Attire and accessories are used to help close this gap but ambiguity resides in the degree of belief in the authenticity of the portrayal. There must be some way to clarify the "appropriate" identity of each other, but how?

The public erotic situation creates an atmosphere of imagery and symbolism that facilitates the exchange of communications between participants in asserting appropriate sexual propensities. Public contexts provide intentional contours within which the dynamic countercurrents of sexual disclosure take place without threatening the face of the individual.

The erotic situation is instrumental in sustaining the symbolic context within which the individual can communicate the necessary prerequisites for sexual interaction. Within this context individuals not only recognize, exchange, complement, and reciprocally sustain the sexual claims of the other, but through the subtle processes of significant gesture and visual communication are able to reinforce their sexual interests, identities, and roles without having to face the threat of painful rejection.

Associated with each identity ideal are sexual, behavioral, anatomical, personality, and role expectations. To suggest symbolically a given identity (through presence in any particular situation, and in dress, mannerisms, behavior, attitude, and physical display) is to seek personal validation as a specific type of individual and an attempt to attain sexual status.

THE CLOSET

The adroit and secret placement of homosexual claims along the edges and peripheries of moral society have been labeled as the "closet" by the gay liberation movement (Humphreys, 1972). The closet refers to a style of life that structures appropriate identities and social action with concomitantly appropriate audiences, or at least sustaining the imagery of such. Societal involvement is classified into heterosexual and homosexual spheres of social participation. It is an attempt to maintain social order by creating social distance between conflicting identities and roles in existing moral categories, often requiring the employment of identity "shields" and game behavior to avoid suspicion (whether real or imagined). An erotic world of communication, both visual and gestural, has evolved by which social reality can be probed and tested as to social requirements and/or permissiveness as one plods through social routine. These probes aid in the definition, projection, and maintenance of what is "gay," what is "straight," and what is "possible."

The closet then is the focal strategy in the relatively easy integration/segregation of gay and straight roles in one's social routine. Its pursuit, however, is an implicit acceptance of conventional notions of social categories and their moral stratification. The homosexual is seen as deviant and stigma-evoking so that the life slot allotted to him is structured in such a way that it does not intrude on public morality or societal sensibilities (for a contrary view, see Sagarin, 1973: 10). The political reality of the dual life results in the reinforcement of a paradoxical circularity of deviance avowal and disavowal, according to the liberationists: homosexual desires and needs —threat of label — avoidance of label (covert claims in public places) — subcultural participation — homosexual identity statement — threat of label — etc.

The gay liberationist sees the closet as a reflection of the moral sentiments of society. It mirrors the negative status that the homosexual occupies and the "abnormal" implications of conceptions of self and social worth (see Kitsuse, 1964, for a discussion of negative definitions and reactions to deviant behavior).

An alternative to the "closet" developed after the Stonewall Riot gave birth to the gay liberation movement (for a history of the early phases of the movement, see Teal, 1971). This small but highly vocal group, no longer tolerant of the deviant status of the homosexual, loudly and actively demand full legitimate recognition for those with different sexual orientations. Coming out of their own closets by discarding secret identities and roles, they not only refuse to slip silently into the shadows when a gay setting is raided, but will audaciously challenge the right for such action to take place.

The activists are not only challenging existing power relationships and the homosexual's deviant status but also actually providing "open" settings as alternatives to the unobtrusive world of the closet. Several organizations have set up clubhouses or community centers that afford homosexuals a place to socialize, not simply in the highly rarified, impersonal atmosphere of the cruise situation like the bars, baths, and toilets (which they are against), but on the basis of one's individuality. They publicly advertise gay activities through the mass media and leaflets, symbolically claiming the legitimacy of a "normal" existence. Yet, in spite of five years of activism they have not succeeded in effecting change in the public erotic world. Why?

Gay activists present a dilemma for the typical covert homosexual. If the closet is a result of the fear of stigmatization, it is the major way in which one's social and sexual life is integrated. It has served faithfully for decades and probably centuries as the way to make "sense" out of conflicting demands and expectations of homosexual desires in a heterosexually defined social world. In short, the activists advocate the end of a style of life that is synonymous with being a homosexual. For the covert homosexual, who has taken great pains to come to terms with a volatile contradiction in social expectations, who has made some adjustment and some sense in living through the dual life, and is able to identify homosexual others through a network of highly emotionally charged silent cues, postures, and other erotic communications, the gauntlet hurled by the activist is patently unpalatable. It offers the annihilation of an extremely sensuous slice of life without replacing it with an equally engrossing alternative. After all, the rarified public homosexual characterizations conjured up in the hesitatingly unfolding, tension-evoking network of gestural significations, so bitterly criticized by the gay activists, are molded by the mutual, fantasy-fed imputations of the players and the social syntax of the situation. Existential contingencies and situational constraints preclude verbal avenues into motivation, intention, identity, and role, freeing the conjecturing individual from a historically confining biography. Momentarily etched on the translucent union of social reality and erotic fantasy, these depersonalized portraits surface in a silent gathering to briefly, but intensely, enact sensuous scripts.

STRANGERS

The scenes of these scripts are constructed out of the same social material as conventional life but assume sexual hues through imaginative anticipations and amorous expectations. Episodal in nature, public erotic characterizations lack a past and a future. The dramatis personae of one episode may be quite something else in another. Contingencies change and with them erotic portrayals and sexual expectations. Awareness contexts shift rapidly, depending on who enters and departs from a situation (see Glaser and Strauss, 1967). Communications accelerate or crumble as negotiations obviate or obliterate imputed personalities. Familiar faces bring safety to a scene but they have no identity until they renew it through silent discourse. Barriers to familiarity require a renegotiated characterization in what is considered a new tryst.

The participant ever remains a stranger, albeit a challenging one.

In point of fact, relations between members of the silent community are perpetually that of conscious strangers. The attitude of the stranger confers an objective perspective through which the participant views ongoing reality as a possible if transient theater of erotic scenes (see Simmel, 1950: 405-407). Such a perspective is adaptable to continuous change — and converging or digressing situational contingencies. It is only in the role of erotic stranger that mutually attracted, but unknown individuals, can touch each other, overcoming the sacred and inviolate nature of the body without making further commitments (see Hall, 1966).

The objective perspective of the stranger becomes part of the daily living assumptions of the public eroticist, which now and again or more sporadically, directs his behavior. That appropriate settings exist, that there are public erotic others with whom to communicate, that communication is not only possible but probable, and that the resulting activities will be successful are the assumptions made by the homosexual (see Garfinkel, 1967: particularly Chapter II). He does not think of the complexities behind his public activities. He does not ask himself if they are possible or different. They are part of the taken-for-granted reality of the individual involved in the "natural attitude of daily living" (Schultz, 1967).

SCENES

If participation is episodal, the "scene" of erotic encounters does not change. The familiar — the routine — serves as both backdrop and exaggerated components of the public erotic world. The street, toilet, park, glory hole, gay bar, pig parlor, or bath represents a setting, a particular type of stage that, given the latitudes and constraints on sexual performances, attract those who prefer this sexual scenario over all others. A combination of factors such as danger, risk of discovery, mystery, quick interaction, odors, sounds, and extravagant visual stimulation create an exotic, erotic fantasy in a surrealistically managed moment. Although some individuals attend many different public oases, there is that "one" scene that really inflames passion. Yet, the "scene" remains very much a part of the mundane world. The gay bath on 28th Street could be simply another business building, given its uninteresting facade, and not-worthy-of-notice clientele. Nothing is more pedestrian than the street or public toilet, and the gay bar — either by secreted locations, or carefully facaded fronts, and certainly by late hour participation — remains inconspicuously conventional (with some exceptions, of course).

MORAL ORDER

That there is an order not only separating but binding together these two, of many, moral worlds can be seen by the great care exercised by the public eroticist as he pursues both his conventional and homosexual pursuits. It is not merely the danger that circumscribes public erotic behavior, but the concern that discovery will destroy the "scene." It is the sense of "adventure," the escalation of pedestrian stuff into a state of erotic tautness, that breath of difference between the abyss and falling over the edge that fire the imagination in public erotic work (for a discussion of the "adventure" in everyday reality, see Lyman and Scott, 1975: Chapter 8). The rhetoric of the gay liberation movement pointedly fails to see this side of covert activity. How can such heights be attained if both worlds collide or if the homosexual world is fully legitimated, no longer requiring intrigue and subterfuge? Conventional identities would flatten the sensuosity in the erotic realm. There would be no need for silence and silent communication, and attendant ambiguity and tension. The erotic world would become an extension of the mundane, grounding soaring flights of erotic fancy into commonplace experiences.

By the same token, the flatness of the everyday world is a

vivid relief for exotic experience. The sheer weight and magnitude of daily routine restores calm and order from "scene" participation. They are inextricably wedded and mutually complementary.

Social order to which the silent community makes only one contribution is not a fabric woven from a singular cloth. It consists of a jumbled, multi-tiered, overlapping series of social realities that manage to mostly co-exist through individual beliefs that there is an order. It is like a distantly admired flowerbed. The whole forms a harmonious and un-differentiated canopy of color. As one draws near, each flower takes on its individual shape and color. With closer inspection, the age and health of the individual flower becomes visible as each bloom traverses the cycle of bud to seed. Lastly, by peering under the mantel of flowers and leaves, an entirely different world struggles for existence. Ants, caterpillars, and an army of other insects busy them-selves with life chores, in a type of antagonistic symbiosis, competing with each other for the garden's favors, some-times enhancing, sometimes destroying the "apparent" harmony of the flowers above.

NOTE

1. See Merle Miller's public confession in *The New York Times*, January 17, 1971.

Appendix A. On the Research Methodology

THE SETTING OF THE STUDY

The large homosexual population of New York City was the deciding factor to conduct the study there. The diversity in subcultural haunts provides a rich cross section of both the public erotic population and erotic meeting areas. However, the size of the homosexual population, diversity of subcultural settings, and the city's expansiveness precluded a study covering the entire urban area.

Some factors indicated that various settings of the city could be omitted from the study without biasing it. For example, several subway toilets in Queens were observed at the commencement of the project. It was discovered that these toilets were of little interest during most of the day. Few individuals used them between rush hours. It was also learned that many individuals who used the Queens' subway settings for erotic activities before and after work, utilize subway and other public settings during the day in Manhattan where they work. Because of work-a-day population concentrations, the Manhattan and downtown Brooklyn subway toilets were more or less busy all the time. This recommended a parsimony in time and effort in data collection.

THE PLACEMENT OF PUBLIC EROTIC ACTIVITIES IN EVERYDAY ROUTINE

The ethnographer's problem concentrated on what settings of the urban area to select, how to organize a research project around them, and what corrective measures, if any, were necessary to assure a representative sample of public erotic activity of the erotic population in commonplace, daily functioning.[1]

Given the definitional criteria of the population, only public homosexual erotic settings within the context of the commonsense notions of these terms were observed. Accessibility is a prime consideration in such notions. The locked toilets in a vast shopping/business plaza located in the center of the city prevents accessibility as do other esoteric settings in the city.[2] Inaccessible to the public at large, such settings were not observed and do not contribute to the data of the study.

AN OPEN SAMPLE

The observer allowed general patterns of urban activity to direct and focus research activities. New York City has gravity points during specific times of the day and specific days of the week. Currents of population tend to flow in certain directions, and by specific conduits of transportation into rather generalized but concentrated areas. Through information obtained from Dr. E (see below), from an early tearoom study of his own, and from homophile groups and direct observation (information gleaned from tearoom walls listing other great "suck spots"; overheard conversations in bars and baths; and tailing public eroticists from one setting to the next), the observer compiled an initial list of erotic settings. The list included public toilets on all major transit lines (at suggested times of maximal activity), parks, beaches, theaters, segments of streets, the notorious trucks, bars, baths, shops, stores, and a host of vacant spaces such as corridors in major building complexes, stairwells, and tunnels that sporadically host public erotic activity.

After initial visits to some of the settings, it was apparent that some offered similar data. Settings were therefore dropped from the list without biasing the data. Also, the observer discovered settings throughout the years of observation that seemed to indicate important additional information, so that additions and subtractions occurred continually throughout the project. Hence, the sample of settings was open-ended.

Public eroticism is a highly volatile activity. One setting may be popular today, but may be of little subsequent interest. Flexibility was required in the study because activity moves from one setting to the next. The observer, for example, stumbled on an erotic incident involving a black man and a white one in a subway toilet. At that point in research, few encounters had been observed involving blacks. The observer, hoping to expand his data in this area, continued to return to this setting, but was continually disappointed. After making a "reading" of the walls, he concluded that the lack of graffiti, and paucity of erotic debris on the floor indicated a rather neutral setting.

Obvious population concentrations in the city suggested placement of research effort. Manhattan is the focus of the commercial, cultural, and entertainment components of the city. Every type of public erotic setting can be found sandwiched within its confines. It was felt that observation within this area would be representative of similar settings in other divisions of the city because heavy flows of population during the work-a-day week originate in the latter. To control for this assumption, similar settings were randomly observed in urban subdivisions. They were found to be no different from those observed in the core area, except for a much slower pace of activity and perhaps a population that reflected the ethnic, racial or occupational nature of the surrounding area.

The cost in time and effort on the observer's part also played a role in the calculations of observation placement. Of the many years of investigation, only one was entirely free — aside from academic pursuits — to pursue the full range of public settings and times, especially very late and isolated phenomena. During the other years, the observer was employed full-time and had to weave observations around his own work-a-day routine.

There were difficulties with the initial sample of settings. References drawn from a certain class or type of individual reflect specific sexual goals. Dr. E was met during one of the observer's initial observations of a bath and was instrumental in compiling the initial list. However, he prefers the western to leather sexual scene, the participants of whom are usually white and middle class. The list of public conveniences he furnished reflected his expectations of sexual others: white, middle class, and leather. Omitted were references to blacks, orientals, Jews, piss-elegance, etc.

Blacks were found in the johns and bars Dr. E recommended, but these participants acted somewhat differently from blacks found in reputedly black settings subsequently developed by the observer. The racially mixed settings were located in predominately white areas and catered to a white population. Because there are toilets that attract a rather homogeneous black population, the choice of attending one setting over another — because all are equally convenient and well-known — is a secure index into the sexual aspirations of the participants and a reflection of the identities with which they associate.

Dissatisfied with the racial characteristics of the original list of settings, the observer branched out into other settings. The observer discovered several black toilets, a black bath, and black bars. The black bath was not observed because of its location in an area known for open hostility to whites — hostility twice experienced by the observer. Public toilets utilized predominately by blacks, some of which were not located in black neighborhoods, were observed on a consistent basis, particularly during the latter years of research.

The original list of settings established one important point immediately. The public erotic population is broadly heterogenous, united only for the purpose of public sexuality and attendant goals.

The heterogeneity of the public erotic population presented an acute challenge. It was important that no special characteristic of any setting, or of its participants, assume a distorting importance from the general population of settings and actors.

A careful selection of types of public settings for observation secured representation of the city's erotic populations. Types of public erotic settings provide a comprehensive range of participants because of whom they attract. For example, the individual who indulges only sporadically in public erotic behavior, or who enjoys extensive heterosexual involvement that does not permit him anything but the most transitory, efficient participation, is found in tearoom activities or spontaneous situations. Those who cannot afford the high price of bars and baths, or who cannot invest much time in homosexual pursuits, engage in tearoom, park, or truck activities. Those who feel uncomfortable with social others that are of a different race or ethnicity do not frequent toilets, bars, or baths where these individuals can be found, but attend settings that assure the presence of few such individuals. As an example, the individual who dislikes blacks will sojourn to Fire Island during the summer months rather than to Riis Park. The former is expensive and mostly white; the latter can be reached by mass transit and is heavily black.

By the same token, bars and some baths have a reputation of attracting types of erotic identities and are frequented for this reason. Individuals who entertain these conceptions of self and identify with such types will attend them in preference to other settings. Leather and piss-elegance never mix.

The sample of homosexual spaces covered in the monograph attempted to include the range of homosexual settings around which different groups of individuals, holding particular self-conceptions of themselves and expectations of others, tend to gather.

While obviousness of erotic identity and intentions is a prerequisite in more sophisticated settings, it is unnecessary and perhaps irrelevant for communications in less structured, more amorphous situations. Thus while such situations provide data as to what is required to lay claim to and maintain a specific situational identity, it simultaneously indicates what elements are not necessary in successfully claiming unconventional identities in other settings. For example, costuming in drag is not a prerequisite in making a successful public homosexual conquest in the toilets, parks, truck stops, transportation hubs, etc., that stretch across the country and abroad. It is vital, however, in leather and piss-elegant establishments.

One type of situation that could not in anyway be consistently observed was the spontaneous encounter. Its unplanned occurrence, lack of structure, loose imputation of deviant identities, and nebulous modes of interaction precluded consistent observation. For the same reasons, the type of participants of these moments could in no way be controlled. Except for two encounters, all participants observed involved two middle class white males. Although only the most fortuitous circumstances led to the observation of spontaneous moments, they could be anticipated in areas of the city that are reputed to be frequented by many homosexuals.

Other variables that could affect the study if not anticipated are age, socio-economic status, ethnicity, and perhaps religion. We have already discussed measures that were employed to increase the number of blacks within the study. Special measures to control for other factors were thought unnecessary because of the range of observations. It is true that some biases exist in specific settings. No one under 18 or 21 is permitted in bars and baths; some toilets are mostly black while many bars and baths tend to be white. Orientals have been observed only in baths and nowhere else. Socio-economic class differentials were inferred from the cost of situational participation (cover minimums, entrance fees, and the cost of drinks), quality of attire, degree of cleanliness, attitude, physical comportment, location of space (good neighborhood or poor), and anecdotal information. When all of these elements are considered and compared to the diversity of settings observed no group seemed excluded.[3]

The observer was caught in many types of crises faced by the public eroticist. These were unplanned experiences, but invaluable for research. The public eroticist is momentarily subject to them on a routine basis. For example, every interruption in public and institutional toilets is a mini-crisis that demands cover and/or recovery tactics. Toilets in a large educational institution, well reputed for great sexual opportunities, suddenly underwent suppression. The observer was intensively questioned by security when he could not produce a student identity card. He was also present during a police raid on a large pig parlor and police raids in two different parks. In addition, the observer was almost robbed and possibly beaten by a gang of black youths in a Brooklyn park.

One last word on the sample of settings used in the study. The pulse of public erotic work depends very much on the pulse of the urban area. During work and school hours, settings in general are comparatively dull. Lunch breaks, class intervals, and leisure hours dramatically quicken the pulse of activity. Common hours of transit to and from work affect the frequency of public erotic activity. The use of types of settings vary with this routine pattern. Since subway and institutional toilets are open for use only during specified hours, hours of utilization are fixed. The intensity of use in turn depends on the urban clock. The observer varied observations accordingly.

Various settings were observed during different days of the seven-day week, catching any differentials in weekday and/or weekend public erotic events and populations. Bars were observed rather consistently during late evening hours because they tend to be late evening phenomena. A few are open during lunch time and cater to a business crowd.

Baths have a lunch crowd and were observed at this time. In general, baths like bars tend to be prolific during the evening hours. All settings that require the mantle of darkness for erotic work were observed at night. Included in this category are parks, trucks, certain streets, and theaters. Beaches require daylight and summer observation and were observed at such times.

METHODS AND STRATEGEMS
OF DATA COLLECTION

The observer quickly discovered that the population of the study is only discernible as such during moments of public homosexual erotic behavior.[4] The peculiar set of communication and interaction techniques employed by the public eroticist produce various problems for data collection, but enhance specific observational strategies.

Several key similarities in the settings observed seemed to contour erotic interaction and have been instrumental in delineating the definitional aspects of the problem and deciding what methodologies to use. The publicness of transactions provides accessibility and observability for both participants and observer. Communications for this reason are restricted to the visual rather than the verbal level in the ritual of identity transformation. The visible erotic topic of communications defines the atypical nature of the interaction. The significant elements that structured data collection was this combination of inaccessible accessibility to the participants and their covert observability.

What does this mean for techniques of data collection? If the individual participants are not only inaccessible to the researcher but also unknown to him except during deviant moments, there are no identifiable public eroticists to talk to before involvement. Because silence prevents communication (verbal), to question anyone during involvement is to lose not only the individual but the situation as well. To approach the departing individual after he has successfully attained orgasm or at least firmly identified himself as a public eroticist through his activities in a subway john, the park, the theater, or beach is to approach a very vulnerable human being. Breaching situational etiquette creates immediate suspicion, fear, and a loss of interest in erotic activities and usually results in flight.

Various gay liberation organizations provide access to a host of individuals who are very happy to submit to interviews. However, the homophile membership draws from a particularly youthful and radical population that does not represent the range of actors found in public erotic settings. Interviewing or questioning a population drawn from gay groups, organizations, bars, and baths biases the data. The membership does not represent the diversity of individuals who are found in public erotic moments who may or may not recognize homosexual inclinations, and who may participate in erotic moments for other than sexual purposes (the hustler, thief, fag-hater, vice cop, and male prostitute).

If justice is to be done to the diversity of erotic populations, and if erotic situations are to be sustained without interruption to prevent research bias, the only methodological tool to come to grips with this kind of behavior is participant observation. This method of data collection focuses research on entire erotic contexts and situations. The range of participants can be observed as they make their contribution to deviant moments. The nexus of events, the combination of action, reaction, and interaction, and the probing and testing in erotic work are best captured by a comprehensive, detailed recording of the circumstances that evoke, sustain, and terminate deviant moments.

The recording of the natural history of deviant moments has several advantages.[5] The natural sphere of everyday life is permitted to exhibit itself in all its complexity, diversity, and contradictions. Rather than entertain preconceived notions of the action involved, directing the observer's interests in one area while perhaps encouraging significant omissions in others, the natural history method dictates that the whole sphere of action is noteworthy — until the observer learns to discern what is significant.

To what degree participant observation? Types of settings varied widely in the degree to which the observer participated. Before discussing them, it should be mentioned that all of the settings shared common obstructions that interfered with tidy data collection. Note-taking was postponed until after the observer's departure from the setting. Because the detail of activity in each setting proved tremendous, typified sketches were constructed to economize time and effort. Gradually, some six months after the project began, the observer only noted what was new to him, rounding out the noted patterns already established.

Returning to the topic of degree of participation, the more tenuous, dangerous, and ambiguous the erotic setting, the more the observer had to participate. Because identities are quite ambiguous during these moments, each must exert himself to counter any doubts of the identity of the other. What does this mean on an operational level?

In those situations that occur spontaneously, the observer had free reign to observe provided he in no way indicated that he was watching. He assumed the role, for example, of the man naturally involved on the street passing from one destination to another. This machination was possible because spontaneous moments usually occur in wide open contexts, providing little evidence of illicit activity. If the participants found themselves under observation, the incident usually abruptly disintegrated. To prevent disintegration if discovered watching, the observer tried to indicate that he was part of the scene and meant no harm. This maneuvering availed him little.

Settings requiring overt proof for inclusion, e.g., the public toilet, were more of a problem for the observer. Humphreys states that the role of "watchqueen" secures a place for the social scientist in the unfolding drama of the tearoom.[6] Perhaps this was possible within the park facility he observed. This observer found the role only partially effective and many times limiting, if not actually disruptive of the situation. Because tearoom settings are spatially dissimilar, it proved effective only in those settings that actually needed a sentinel. The role tends to be superfluous in subway toilets that have no windows. In fact, it proved annoying for those who wanted to get involved. Public parks, the trucks, certain streets, and the pier, all late night phenomena, make the role ludicrous. Every man is on his own in such places.

No rigid role-play is really required in public erotic settings. The public eroticist often manipulates conventional expectations in pursuing his interests. The use of the urinal for such purposes has been described above. Similar manipulation was learned by the observer and used extensively.

One problem for the observer who has been accepted as part of an erotic situation is maintaining social distance from those that are being observed. No matter how he tries to prevent it, an erotic approach will inevitably occur. Not only must the observer avoid exhibiting signs of embarrassment, chagrin, or fear, he must handle the rejection appropriately — within the context of the situation and without embarrassing the interested party if the situation is to remain unaffected.

To elaborate on all the roles assumed by the researcher during field trips would take a volume in itself. He found that almost any setting afforded a host of roles conducive to inclusion in the setting's activities, while maintaining sufficient distance from the host subjects. His most important assets were the ability to discern appropriate roles and how to manipulate a self-presentation that encouraged acceptance while maintaining social distance.[7] Although increasing exposure rewarded the researcher with increasing adeptness, he was a bungling beginner at the commencement of this project and would have failed in his undertaking had it not been for several fortuitous events that rescued him from ignorance.

THE PUBLIC EROTIC EDUCATION
OF THE RESEARCHER

At the beginning of the research project the researcher knew very little about the public erotic marketplace. He did not know the extent of public homosexual eroticism or where it was to be found. He was shockingly deficient in the knowledge of what it consisted and how to recognize the subtle, tenuous initial cues that lead to its fruition.

Several fortuitous circumstances occurred that resolved these serious inadequacies. The most important was the observer's introduction to Dr. E. During the first attempt in observing a homosexual bath in 1969, the lead for which was furnished by a now deceased co-worker, the observer met an individual who later identified himself as a teacher in an out-of-town college.

Dr. E was extremely helpful in not only educating the observer, but in relating the full range of knowledge he had of public erotic settings. Later on, when the observer got to know Dr. E better, an exchange was made whereby Dr. E utilized the observer's apartment on weekends for his New York City erotic forays provided he give the observer not only accounts of his experiences and reports of new public settings, but also tours of such settings.

Dr. E is a virtuoso of public eroticism. Dedicated to discovering the new and interesting, he keeps abreast of the most recent changes in public erotic settings, including bars, baths, parks, beaches, book shops, pig parlors, and other niches of interest. His constant search for the new and exciting leads him into the widest possible range of sexual settings and pursuits. He faithfully informed the observer of his activities and reported all the new settings he found. As a consequence, the observer often knew of changes in the public sexual marketplace before most of its regular participants. As an example, the observer was one of the first visitors to the pig parlor. The observer would never have located or been admitted to them without Dr. E's sponsorship.

Dr. E was helpful in providing valuable insights into situational activities. He accompanied the observer on several field trips, pointing out many subtleties that the observer simply did not see. He also relocated twice during the research period. He gave the observer an escorted tour of each city's erotic underground. This data was valuable for comparative purposes with New York City. Dr. E's active assistance concluded approximately two years before the research in order to devote himself to a monogamous, emotional union.

Another fortuitous event that proved to be a boon for the research project was the Stonewall Riot and the birth and growth of the gay liberation movement. Unaware of the riot, the observer first learned of the movement when GAA (Gay Activist Alliance) advertised itself in a local newspaper. The observer attended the third meeting of the group sometime in December, 1969, and attended at least one general meeting a month thereafter for three years. He sporadically attended committee meetings during the week, participated in many marches and demonstrations, and got to know the leaders of the group quite well. Although the initial membership of the group was small during the fledgling months (approximately 20-30 regular attenders), it grew to several hundred within a year. News, problems, information, and hundreds of individuals with whom to speak and question were concentrated in one location. The organization acted as a switchboard of current information and a storehouse of data on gay life for not only the immediate urban area but for the country as a whole. Changes in the gay scene, including public erotic locales and their harrassment, were received and disseminated quickly. The organization continually attracted an interchange of individuals from areas outside the urban area, providing first-hand information on the gay scene in distant areas. The observer's participation in several GAA-sponsored demonstrations provided dramatic first-hand experience of the hostility homosexuals encounter from the general public.

The publication of a west coast homophile newspaper also contributed to data gathering. By exclusively dealing with homosexual problems and news in concentrated form, it provided much information that would have been very difficult and time consuming to obtain by other means. It too was utilized extensively.

NOTES

1. The empirical undertaking germinating in the slow and random introduction to the subculture by the observer has been guided by the helpful words of Glaser and Strauss (1967: 34), "Our approach, allowing substantive concepts and hypotheses to emerge first, on their own, enables the analyst to ascertain which, if any, existing formal theory may help him generate substantive theories. He can then be more faithful to his data, rather than forcing it to fit a theory. He can be more objective and less theoretically biased."

2. These toilets are locked for the purpose of keeping out the general public since they are intended for employee use only. Another example of inaccessibility to the general erotic population is the cruise ship that departs at 2:00 a.m. from P-town, and sails past the three-mile limit to provide safe orgies for homosexual passengers.

3. This includes two orthodox Jews, attired in ethnic dress, actively engaged in erotic posturing in toilets.

4. Unlike Humphreys (1970) who had recourse to the nonhomosexual characteristics of park toilet participants through license plate numbers of their vehicles, no avenue existed by which the observer could further pursue the backgrounds of his subjects.

5. For a definition of "natural" and "naturalism" as utilized in this section, see Matza, 1969: Chapter I.

6. Humphreys, 1970: 16-45.

7. In many situations the observer enacted many roles: an unaware co-passenger on the subway, an uninterested gay in the toilet, voyeur, and egocentric in the bath. The ease with which he did so and the level of observation without detection reveals the vulnerability of the "silent community." The charades were necessitated by the delicate nature of the unfolding dramas and the threat the observer represented if the slightest indication of his identity were known.

References

REFERENCES

The Advocate, 4:13, August 19 — September 1, 1970.

_____ 61, June 9-22, 1971.

_____ 96, October 11, 1972.

_____ 168, July 16, 1975.

Ardrey, Robert. *The Territorial Imperative.* N.Y.: Atheneum, 1966.

Becker, Howard S. *Outsiders: Studies in the Sociology of Deviance.* N.Y.: Free Press, 1968.

Berger, Peter L., and Thomas Luckmann. *The Social Construction of Reality.* Garden City, N.Y.: Anchor Books, Doubleday, 1967.

Bowers, Faubian. "Homosexual: Living the Life," *Saturday Review,* LV:7, February 12, 1972.

Brownell, Baker. *The Human Community: Its Philosophy and Practice for A Time of Crisis.* N.Y.: Harper & Row, 1950.

Churchill, Wainwright. *Homosexual Behavior Among Males.* N.Y.: Hawthorn Books, 1967.

Cohen, Albert. *Deviance and Control.* Englewood Cliffs, N.J.: Prentice-Hall, 1966.

Cooley, Charles Horton. *Human Nature and the Social Order.* N.Y.: Schocken Books, 1964.

Fisher, Peter. *The Gay Mystique: The Myth and Reality of Male Homosexuality.* N.Y.: Stein & Day, 1971.

Gagnon, John H., and William Simon. "Homosexuality: The Formulation of a Sociological Perspective," *Approaches to Deviance,* J. Lefton, J. Skipper, and C. McCoghy, eds. N.Y.: Appleton-Century-Croft, 1968.

Garfinkel, Harold. *Studies in Ethnomethodology.* Englewood Cliffs, N.J.: Prentice-Hall, 1967.

Gay, 3:67, January, 1972.

Glaser, Barney G., and Anselm Strauss. "Awareness Contexts and Social Interaction," *Symbolic Interaction,* Jerome G. Manus and Bernard N. Meltzer, eds. Boston: Allyn and Bacon, 1967.

_____ . *The Discovery of Grounded Theory, Strategies for Qualitative Research.* Chicago: Aldine, 1967.

Goffman, Erving. *Interaction Ritual.* Garden City, N.Y.: Anchor Books, Doubleday, 1967.

_____ . Behavior in Public Places. N.Y.: Free Press, 1963.

_____ . *Stigma.* Englewood Cliffs, N.J.: Prentice-Hall, 1963.

_____ . *Encounters.* N.Y.: Bobbs-Merrill, 1961.

_____ . *The Presentation of Self in Everyday Life.* Garden City, N.Y.: Anchor Books, Doubleday, 1959.

Goldstein, Richard. "S & M: The Dark Side of Gay Liberation," *The Village Voice.* XX:27, July 7, 1975.

Hall, Edward T. *The Hidden Dimension.* Garden City, N.Y.: Doubleday, 1966.

_____ . *The Silent Language.* Garden City, N.Y.: Doubleday, 1959.

Hoffman, Martin. *The Gay World.* N.Y.: Basic Books, 1968.

Humphreys, Laud. *Out of the Closets.* Englewood Cliffs, N.J.: Prentice-Hall, 1972.

_____ . *Tearoom Trade.* Chicago: Aldine, 1970.

Hunter, John Francis. *The Gay Insider, USA.* N.Y.: Stonehill Publishing, 1972.

_____ . *The Gay Insider.* N.Y.: The Traveller's Companion Inc., Olympia Press, 1971.

Kitsuse, John I. "Societal Reaction to Deviant Behavior: Problems of Theory and Method," *The Other Side,* Howard S. Becker, ed. N.Y.: Free Press, 1964.

Lemert, Edwin. *Human Deviance, Social Problems, and Social Control.* Englewood Cliffs, N.J.: Prentice-Hall, 1967.

Leznoff, Maurice, and William A. Westley. "The Homosexual Community," *The Problem of Homosexuality in Modern Society,* Hendrik M. Ruitenbeek, ed. N.Y.: E.P. Dutton, 1963.

Lofland, John. *Deviance and Identity.* Englewood Cliffs, N.J.: Prentice-Hall, 1969.

Lofland, Lyn H. *A World of Strangers.* N.Y.: Basic Books, 1973.

Lyman, Stanford M., and Marvin B. Scott. *The Drama of Social Reality.* N.Y.: Oxford University Press, 1975.

_____ . *A Sociology of the Absurd.* N.Y.: Meredith Corporation, 1970.

Marks, Edward, and Lloyd J. Papnerno. *Criminal Law in New York.* Amityville, N.Y.: Acme Law Book, 1967.

Matza, David. *Becoming Deviant.* Englewood Cliffs, N.J.: Prentice-Hall, 1969.

McCall, George J., and J. L. Simmons. *Identities and Interactions: An Examinator of Human Associations in Everyday Life.* New York: Free Press of Glencoe, 1966.

Mead, George Herbert. *Mind, Self, and Society.* Charles W. Morris, ed. Chicago Press, 1934.

Merton, Robert K. "Social Problems and Sociological Theory," *Contemporary Social Problems,* Robert K. Merton and Robert A. Nisbet, eds. N.Y.: Harcourt and Brace, 1971.

_____. *Social Theory and Social Structure.* Toronto, Ontario: Free Press, 1949.

Mills, C. Wright. "Situated Actions and Vocabularies of Motive," *Symbolic Interaction,* Jerome G. Manus and Bernard N. Meltzer, eds. Boston: Allyn and Bacon, 1967.

Milner, Christine and Richard. *Black Players, The Secret World of Black Pimps.* Boston: Little, Brown, 1972.

Newton, Esther. *Mother Camp: Female Impersonators In America.* Englewood Cliffs, N.J.: Prentice-Hall, 1972.

Parsons, Talcott. *The Social System.* N.Y.: Free Press, 1951.

Ponte, Meredith R. "Life in a Parking Lot: An Ethnography of a Homosexual Drive-In," *Deviance: Field Studies and Self-disclosures,* Jerry Jacobs, ed. Palo Alto, CA: National Press Books, 1974.

Rechy, John. *Numbers.* N.Y.: Grove Press, 1967.

_____. *City of Night.* N.Y.: Grove Press, 1963.

Reisman, David. *The Lonely Crowd.* New Haven: Yale University Press, 1950.

Reiss, Albert J. "The Social Integration of Queers and Peers," *Deviance, The Interactionist Perspective,* Earl Rubington and Martin S. Weinberg, eds. London: Macmillan, 1968.

Sagarin, Edward. "The Good Guys, the Bad Guys, and the Gay Guys," *Contemporary Sociology,* 2:1, January, 1973.

Scheflen, Albert E. *Body Language and Social Order.* Englewood Cliffs, N.J.: Prentice-Hall, 1972.

Scherer, Jacqueline. *Contemporary Community, Sociological Illusion or Reality?* London: Tavistock, 1972.

Schofield, Michael. *Sociological Aspects of Homosexuality.* Boston: Little, Brown, 1965.

Schutz, Alfred. *Collected Papers: The Problem of Social Reality.* I. Maurice Natanson, ed. The Hague: Martinus Nijhoff, 1967.

_____. *Collected Papers: Studies in Social Theory.* II, Arvid Brodersen, ed. The Hague: Martinus Nijhoff, 1964.

Schwartz, Michael, and Sheldon Stryker. *Deviance, Selves, and Others.* Washington, D.C.: The Arnold and Caroline Rose Monograph Series Sociology, American Sociological Association, 1970.

Shur, Edwin. *Crimes Without Victims.* Englewood Cliffs, N.J.: Prentice-Hall, 1965.

Simmel, Georg. *The Sociology of Georg Simmel.* Kurt H. Wolff, ed. N.Y.: Free Press, 1950.

Stone, Gregory P. "Appearance and the Self," *Human Behavior and Social Process,* Arnold Rose, ed. Boston: Houghton Mifflin, 1962.

Strauss, Anselm. *Mirrors and Masks.* Chicago: Free Press, 1959.

Sumner, William Graham. *Folkways.* Boston: Ginn and Company, 1906.

Teal, Don. *The Gay Militants.* N.Y.: Stein and Day, 1971.

Time, 106:10, September 8, 1975.

Warren, Carol A. B. *Identity & Community in the Gay World.* N.Y.: A Wiley-Interscience Publication, John Wiley & Sons, 1974.

Weinberg, Martin S., and Colin J. Williams. *Male Homosexuality, Their Problems and Adaptations.* N.Y.: Oxford University Press, 1974.

Weitman, Sasha R. "Intimacies: Notes Toward a Theory of Social Inclusion and Exclusion," *People in Places, The Sociology of the Familiar,* Arnold Birenbaum and Edward Sagarin, eds. N.Y.: Praeger, 1973.

West, D. J. *Homosexuality.* Chicago: Aldine, 1967.

Winick, Charles, and Paul M. Kinsie. *The Lively Commerce, Prostitution in the United States.* Chicago: Quadrangle Books, 1971.

About the Author

EDWARD DELPH received a B.A. in Economics in 1965 from Queens College (CUNY) and his Ph.D. in Sociology from the New School for Social Research in 1976. Ever-fascinated with the social diversity of urban areas, he has worked in the past with narcotic addicts and minority groups in "ghetto areas" and is currently involved with emotionally disturbed youths and delinquent juveniles.